11/30/2014

FINANCIAL REPORTING

About The Author

Dr. David Ackah was born in the Western part of Ghana, precisely Egyambra in the Ahanta West District. He had his basic and secondary education from Egyambra Basic Education, and Esiama Secondary School.

He then obtains Diploma in Economics and Business Management from Colorado Technical University, and Community College of Southern Nevada. Dr. David Ackah again continues his education to University College of Management Studies - UCOMS to read BSc Accounting, as life goes on, he had an admission to study at Atlantic International University at Hawaii precisely Honolulu in USA and Colorado Technical University to read Master of Science (MSc) and Master of Philosophy (M.Phil.) in Economics, with his hard working, he had 3.98 GPA score after his Master of Science in Economics, with this, he again obtain an admission with automatic enrolment to study Doctor of Philosophy in Economics.

Dr. Ackah also studies other professional course from the following institutions: Managing and Marketing Sales Association (MAMSA in Cherish England), Standard Diploma in Sales Management, Institute of Commercial Management (ICM in UK), Diploma in Marketing, and Institute of Export and Shipping Management (IESM in Ghana) Diploma in Marketing & Salesmanship

Dr. Ackah has work with many companies like Tobinco Pharmaceutical Ltd as Marketing Manager in Takoradi, Nutraculture Indian Pharma as Country Manager in Ghana, and Pharmanova Ltd as a Regional Marketing Manager and Teaches in many Colleges, and Secondary schools.

Currently He is a Lecturer in Kwame Nkrumah University of Science Technology, Uniworld University College, and the CEO of Regaro Group of Companies

DEDICATION

I dedicate this Book to God for his love and mercy throughout my traveling on schooling period. I again dedicate this book to my one only love Mrs Makafui Ackah, a lecturer at Accra Poly.

ACKNOWLEDGEMENT

I first and foremost express my love to God for his blessings on me every day during and after the work, and also my old school lectures for the support to me.

And also to my lovely wife Makafui Ackah for her advice and support I really appreciate it

CHAPTER ONE
NATURE OF FINANCIAL REPORTING

Financial Reporting

Financial reporting refers to the reporting of the financial activities of a business, or other entity, to stakeholders of the entity or business. The stakeholders are often referred to as 'users.'

The reports produced for the users are the end product of a financial reporting, or accounting, system. This involves the recording and summarising of the business or entity's transactions and events so that the financial activities can be reported in a format that is useful to the stakeholders of the business or entity.

In order to understand the financial reporting process it is important to consider:

- the context and purpose of financial reporting,
- the importance of a financial reporting framework,
- the design of financial reporting systems,
- how the financial systems are controlled, and
- how to interpret financial reports.

CONSOLIDATED FINANCIAL STATEMENTS

Group

A group exists where one entity, the parent, has control over another entity, the subsidiary. In accordance with IFRS 10 Consolidated Financial Statements control consists of three components:

- Power over the investee, which is normally exercised through the majority of voting rights (i.e. owning more than 50% of the equity shares).
- Exposure or rights to variable returns from involvement (e.g. a dividend).
- The ability to use power over the investee to affect the amount of investor returns. This is regarded as a crucial determinant in deciding whether or not control is exercised.

Requirement to prepare consolidated financial statements

If one company controls another then IFRS 10 requires that a single set of consolidated financial statements be prepared to reflect the financial performance and position of the group as one combined entity. This reflects the fact that the investment of the parents' shareholders is now tied up in more than one entity. Their returns and the stability of their investment now reflect the performance and position of both entities.

In order to make informed decisions about their investment, shareholders would need to read and interpret the financial statements of both companies. If there were more than one subsidiary company this could become quite complex for shareholders. To this end one set of financial statements is prepared where the revenues, expenses, assets and liabilities of the parent and subsidiary are combined for ease of understanding and analysis.

Associates

IAS 28 Accounting for Investments in Associates and Joint Ventures defines an associate as 'an entity over which the investor has significant influence and that is neither a subsidiary nor an interest in a joint venture.'

Significant influence

Significant influence is the power to participate in the financial and operating policy decisions of the investee but is not control or joint control over those policies.
Significant influence is assumed with a shareholding of 20% to 50%.

Accounting for associates

Associates are accounted for using the 'equity method,' whereby the investment is initially recorded at cost and adjusted thereafter for the post-acquisition change in the investor's share of net assets of the associate. In other words the value of the investment is the cost plus the group's share of the associates profits and losses.
The effect of this is that the **statement of financial position** of the group includes a single 'investments in associates' line within non-current assets that includes their share of the assets and liabilities of any associate. This is calculated as follows:

	$000
Cost of investment	X
Share of post-acquisition profits	X
Less: impairment losses	(X)
Less: group share of unrealised profits (when the parent is the seller)	(X)
	X

The consolidated income statement of the group includes a single 'share of profit of associates' line which includes their share of any associate's profit after tax.
Note: in order to equity account, the parent company must already be producing consolidated financial statements (i.e. it must already have at least one subsidiary).

Trading with the associate

Generally the associate is considered to be outside the group. Therefore any sales or purchases between group companies and the associate are not normally eliminated and will remain part of the consolidated figures in the income statement.
Instead it is normal practice to adjust for the group share of any unrealised profit in inventory.

Dividends from associates

Dividends from associates are excluded from the consolidated income statement; the group share of the associate's profit after tax for the year is included instead.

Simple investments

Where an entity invests in the shares of another entity but acquires neither control, nor significant influence this is referred to as a 'simple' or 'trade' investment. In this case the investment is carried as an intangible non-current asset on the statement of financial position and any dividends received are reflected in the income statement.

FAIR VALUES

IFRS 13 para 9 defines fair value as:

"The price that would be received to sell an asset or paid to transfer a liability in an orderly transaction between market participants at the measurement date." i.e. it is an exit price.

Fair values in consolidated financial statements

To ensure that an accurate figure is calculated for goodwill:

- The consideration paid for a subsidiary must be accounted for at fair value. Not all consideration is for cash; other non-cash elements (such as share exchanges) must be valued appropriately,
- The subsidiary's identifiable assets and liabilities acquired must be accounted for at their fair values in order to work out the difference between their value and the amount paid for them.

The need to account on a fair value basis reflects the fact that the statement of financial position often values items (mainly non-current assets) at their historic cost less depreciation. This could mean the book value of assets (or carrying value) is vastly different to their current market values, particularly in the case of assets that tend to appreciate in value, such as land and buildings.

The subsidiary's identifiable assets and liabilities are included in the consolidated accounts at their fair values for the following reasons.

- Consolidated accounts are prepared from the perspective of the group, rather than from the perspectives of the individual companies. The book values of the subsidiary's assets and liabilities are largely irrelevant, because the consolidated accounts must reflect their cost to the group (i.e. to the parent), not their original cost to the subsidiary. The cost to the group is their fair value at the date of acquisition.
- Purchased goodwill is the difference between the value of an acquired entity and the aggregate of the fair values of that entity's identifiable assets and liabilities. If fair values are not used, the value of goodwill will be meaningless.

How to include fair values in consolidation workings

(1)Adjust both columns of the net asset working to bring the net assets to fair value at acquisition and reporting date.

This will ensure that the fair value of net assets is carried through to the goodwill and non-controlling interest calculations.

	At acquisition	At reporting date
	$000	$000
Ordinary share capital	X	X
Retained earnings	X	X
Fair value adjustments	X	X
	X	X

The fair value adjustment represents the amount required to adjust the relevant item from their current carrying value in the SoFP to their identified fair value.

(2) At the reporting date make the adjustment on the face of the **SoFP** when adding across assets and liabilities.

GOODWILL

The value of a company purchased will normally exceed the value of its net assets. The difference is goodwill. This represents assets not shown in the statement of financial position of the acquired company such as the reputation of the business, brand and the experience of employees.

Goodwill arises because the investor would rather buy a ready made and established business than buy the individual components and set up the business themselves from nothing.

Fair value

When calculating goodwill (and non-controlling interests) the fair valuemethod is used. This means that amounts are not calculated merely at their reported book value.

Goodwill is the difference between the amount paid to acquire a shareholding and the value of the assets acquired. However, the amount paid is rarely a simple cash transaction. With large companies shares are often purchased for cash plus an additional payment that is deferred into the future. Often the deferred payments are contingent upon achieving certain performance targets. Alternatively shares are swapped, i.e. a company purchases shares in a subsidiary in exchange for shares in their own company. All of these elements of the 'consideration' have to be valued in today's monetary terms.

The value of the shareholding must also be considered. The net assets are usually calculated by totalling the assets reported on the SoFP and deducting liabilities. The book values, however, often do not reflect their true market value. This is most common with property, plant and equipment. Property often appreciates in value, whereas in the financial statements of some companies it is stated at historic depreciated cost. Therefore the fair value of all assets and liabilities must be determined.

INTRA-GROUP TRADING

Types of intra-group trading

The parent (P) and their subsidiary (S) may well trade with each other during a financial period, leading to the following potential issues to be dealt with:

- receivables and payables in P and S that effectively cancel each other out
- sales and purchases in P and S that effectively cancel each other out
- dividends paid by the subsidiary recognised as income by the parent. Again the net effect of this to the group is zero.
- unrealised profits on sales of inventory between the parent and the subsidiary (to help you understand this concept consider this question; can you make a profit if your right hand sells goods to your left hand? Obviously not and for the same reason a group cannot make profit when one part of the group sells goods to another part).

Current Accounts
If P and S trade with each other than this will probably be done on credit leading to:
- a receivables (current) account in one company's SoFP
- a payables (current) account in the other company's SoFP.

These amounts should not be consolidated because the group would end up with a receivable to itself and a payable to itself.

They are therefore cancelled (contra'd) against each other in the consolidated statement of financial position.

Sales and Purchases
The effect of intra-group trading must be eliminated from the consolidated income statement. Such trading will be included in the sales revenue of one group company and the purchases of another.
- Consolidated sales revenue = P's revenue + S's revenue – intra-group sales.
- Consolidated cost of sales = P's COS + S's COS – intra-group purchases

Unrealised Profit
Profits made by members of a group on transactions with other group members are:
- recognised in the accounts of the individual companies concerned, but
- in terms of the group as a whole, such profits are unrealised and must be eliminated from the consolidated accounts (remember you cannot make profits if your right hand sells goods to your left!).

Such unrealised profits arise when one group company sells good to another group company and those goods have not been sold on externally by the end of the year. They are therefore known as unrealised profits held in inventory.

Intra-group trading and unrealised profit in inventory
When one group company sells goods to another a number of adjustments may be needed.
- Current accounts must be cancelled (see above).
- Where goods are still held by a group company at the reporting date, any unrealised profit must be cancelled.
- Inventory must be included at original cost to the group.

Adjustments for unrealised profit in inventory
(1). Determine the value of closing inventory still held within the group at the reporting date that are the result of intra-group trading.
(2). Use either the profit mark-up or margin to calculate how much of that value represents profit earned by the selling company.
(3.)Make one of the following adjustments:

If the seller is the parent company, the profit element is included in the holding company's accounts and relates entirely to the controlling group.
Adjustment required:
Dr Group retained earnings
Cr Group inventory

If the seller is the subsidiary, the profit element is included in the subsidiary company's accounts and relates partly to the group, partly to non-controlling interests (if any).
Adjustment required:
Dr Subsidiary cost of sales (and therefore their retained earnings in the net asset working)
Cr Group inventory

THE CONSOLIDATED INCOME STATEMENT
The consolidated income statement presents the financial performance of group companies (i.e. parent and subsidiaries under common control) in one, single statement.

The Basic Principles
The consolidated income statement follows the same basic principles as the consolidated statement of financial position. The volumes of adjustments are, however, fewer. The steps for consolidating the income statements are as follows:
(1)Add together the revenues and expenses of the parent and the subsidiary.
If the subsidiary is acquired part way through the year all the revenues and expenses of the subsidiary must be time apportioned during the consolidation process.
(2)Eliminate intra-group sales and purchases.
(3)Eliminate unrealised profit held in closing inventory relating to intercompany trading.
(4)Calculate the profits attributable to the non-controlling interests.
After the net profit for the year the split of profit between amounts attributable to the equity holders of the group and the non-controlling interests (to reflect ownership) is shown.

Non-controlling interest
This is calculated as:

NCI % × subsidiary's profit after tax	X
Less:	
NCI % × PURP (when the sub is the seller only)	(X)
	X

Illustration

The income statements for P and S for the year ended 31 August 20X4 are shown below. P acquired 75% of the ordinary share capital of S several years ago.

	P
	$000
Revenue	1,200
Cost of sales	(1,080)
Gross profit	120
Administrative expenses	(75)
Profit before tax	45
Tax	(15)
Profit for the year	30

The consolidated income statement of P group for the year ended 31 August 20X4

	$000
Revenue (1,200 + 400)	1,600
Cost of sales (1,080 + 360)	(1,440)
Gross profit	160
Administrative expenses (75 + 30)	(105)
Profit before tax	55
Tax (15 + 6)	(21)
Profit for the year	34
Attributable to:	
Group (bal fig)	33
Non-controlling interest (W1)	1
	34

(W1) Non-controlling interest

NCI share of subsidiary profit for the year (NCI% x sub's profit for the year)
25% x $4,000 = $1,000

THE CONSOLIDATED STATEMENT OF FINANCIAL POSITION

The basic method of preparation

- the assets and liabilities of the parent and the subsidiary are added together on a line-by-line basis.
- The investment shown in the parent's SoFP (i.e. the investment in the subsidiary) is replaced by a goodwill figure.
- The share capital and share premium balances are not added together; only the balances related to the parent are used in the consolidation. This reflects the fact that the consolidated SoFP shows all of the assets and liabilities under the control of the parent entity.
- The amount attributable to non-controlling interests (i.e. the other shareholders where the parent owns less than 100% of the ordinary share capital) is calculated and shown separately on the face of the consolidated SoFP.
- The group share of the subsidiary's profit is calculated and added to overall group retained earnings.

THE MECHANICS OF CONSOLIDATION

The group structure

This is where you establish whether there is a parent-subsidiary relationship (i.e. does the parent have control?). It is important to consider all aspects of control as well as percentage shareholding. You do need to identify the percentage shareholding of the parent and the non-controlling interest in order to prepare the remaining workings. You will also need to be aware of the date control was achieved.

Net assets of subsidiary

	At date of acquisition $	At the reporting date $
Share capital	X	X
Share premium	X	X
Revaluation reserve	X	X
Retained earnings	X	X
	X	X

The total of share capital and share premium from the subsidiary statement of financial position should be unchanged at both the date of acquisition and the reporting date.

Goodwill

	$
Fair value (FV) of consideration paid	X
FV of non-controlling interest (NCI) at acquisition	X
	X

Less:

FV of net assets at acquisition	(X)
Goodwill on acquisition	X

Non-controlling interest

FV of NCI at acquisition	X
NCI share of post-acquisition reserv	X
	X

Group retained earnings

	$
Parent's retained earnings (100%)	X
Parent's % of subsidiary's post-acquisition retained earnings	X
	X

Pre-acquisition profits are the retained earnings of the subsidiary which exist at the date when it is acquired. These profits belong to the previous shareholders as they were earned under their ownership. The new parent cannot lay claim to these profits so they are excluded from group retained earnings.

Post-acquisition profits are those profits recognised in retained earnings by the subsidiary at the year-end but earned since the new parent purchased their shareholding. As these were earned under the ownership of the new parent an appropriate percentage (based upon the parent's % ownership) can be recognised in group retained earnings.

Illustration
In order to illustrate the various workings involved in a consolidated statement of financial position we will use the example of D group.
The statements of financial position of D and J as at 31 December 20X8 are included below:

	D	J
	$	$
Non-current assets:		
Property, plant & equipment	85,000	18,000
Investments:		
Shares in J	60,000	
	145,000	
	160,000	84,000
Current assets		

	305,000	102,000

Equity:

Ordinary $1 shares	65,000	20,000
Share premium	35,000	10,000
Retained earnings	70,000	25,000
	170,000	55,000
Current liabilities	135,000	47,000
	305,000	102,000

D acquired an 80% holding in J on 1 January 20X8. At this date J's retained earnings stood at $20,000. On this date, the fair value of the non-controlling shareholding in J was $12,500.

The consolidated statement of financial position of D Group as at 31 December 20X8

Non-current assets	$
Goodwill (W3)	22,500
PPE (85,000 + 18,000)	103,000
Current assets (160,000 + 84,000)	244,000
	369,500

Equity	
Share capital	65,000
Share premium	35,000
Group retained earnings (W5)	74,000
Non-controlling interest (W4)	13,500
	187,500
Current liabilities (135,000 + 47,000)	182,000
	369,500

<u>**Workings**</u>

(W1) Group structure

(W2) Net assets of J

	At date of acquisition	At reporting date
Share capital	20,000	20,000
Share premium	10,000	10,000
Retained earnings	20,000	25,000
Net assets	50,000	55,000

(W3) Goodwill

FV of consideration paid	60,000
FV of NCI at acquisition	12,500
	72,500
Less:	
FV of net assets at acquisition (W2)	(50,000)
Goodwill on acquisition (to SoFP)	22,500

(W4) Non-controlling interests

FV of NCI at acquisition (as in W3)	12,500
NCI share of post-acquisition reserves (W2)	1,000
$(20\% \times (55,000 - 50,000))$	
	13,500

(W5) Group retained earnings

100% D's retained earnings	70,000
80% J post-acquisition retained earnings	4,000
$(80\% \times \$(55,000 - 50,000) \text{ (W2)})$	
	74,000

CHAPTER TWO
CONTROLLING THE FINANCIAL REPORTING SYSTEM

Overview

It is vital that the information provided in the financial statements is consistent with the qualitative characteristics of financial information. One of these if 'faithful representation' which requires that information be free from error. It is therefore vital that controls are built into the financial reporting system to reduce the risk of error in the financial statements. Two of the key controls are:

- preparing and reconciling control accounts, and
- preparing a trial balance.

Once these processes have been completed and any errors corrected the final financial statements can be prepared from the financial data.

BANK RECONCILIATIONS

Introduction

The objective of bank reconciliation is to reconcile the difference between:

- the cash book balance, i.e. the business' record of their bank account, and
- the bank statement balance, i.e. the bank's record of the bank account.

The cash book is the double entry record of cash and bank balances contained within the nominal ledger accounting system. It is, in effect, the cash control account.

Note that debits and credits are reversed in bank statements because the bank will be recording the transaction from its point of view, in accordance with the business entity concept.

Reasons to prepare a bank reconciliation statement

The cash book records all transactions with the bank. The bank statement records all the bank's transactions with the business.

The contents of the cash book should be exactly the same as the record provided by the bank in the form of a bank statement, and therefore the business' records should correspond with the bank statement.

This is in fact so, but with three important provisos:

- The ledger account maintained by the bank is the opposite way round to the cash book. This is because the bank records balances from their perspective. Therefore if a client has a positive bank balance the bank would display this as a credit balance because they have a liability to pay it back to the client. If the client is overdrawn this would be shown as a debit because the bank are owed a repayment from the client.
- Timing differences must inevitably occur. A cheque payment is recorded in the cash book when the cheque is despatched. The bank only records such a cheque when it is paid by the bank, which may be several days later.
- Items such as interest may appear on the bank statement but are not recorded in the cash book as the business is unaware that they have arisen.

The existence of the bank statement provides an important check on the most vulnerable of a company's assets – cash. However, the differences referred to above make it essential to reconcile the balance on the ledger account with that of the bank statement.

Differences between the bank statement and the cash book

When attempting to reconcile the cash book with the bank statement, there are three differences between the cash book and bank statement:

- unrecorded items
- timing differences
- errors

Unrecorded items

These are items which arise in the bank statements before they are recorded in the cash book. Such 'unrecorded items' may include:

- interest
- bank charges
- dishonoured cheques.

They are not recorded in the cash book simply because the business does not know that these items have arisen until they see the bank statement.

Timing differences:

These items have been recorded in the cash book, but due to the bank clearing process have not yet been recorded in the bank statement:

- Outstanding/unpresented cheques (cheques sent to suppliers but not yet cleared by the bank).
- Outstanding/uncleared lodgements (cheques received by the business but not yet cleared by the bank).

The bank statement balance needs to be adjusted for these items:

	$
Balance per bank statement	X
Less: Outstanding/unpresented cheques	(X)
Add: Outstanding/uncleared lodgements	X
	───
Balance per cash book (revised)	X

Errors in the cash book

The business may make a mistake in their cash book. The cash book balance will need to be adjusted for these items.

Errors in the bank statement

The bank may make a mistake, e.g. record a transaction relating to a different person within our business' bank statement. The bank statement balance will need to be adjusted for these items.

OUTSTANDING PAYMENTS AND RECEIPTS

Outstanding or unpresented cheques

Suppose a cheque relating to a payment to a supplier of a company is written, signed and posted on 29 March. It is also entered in the cash book on the same day. By the time the supplier has received the cheque and paid it into his bank account, and by the time his bank has gone through the clearing system, the cheque does not appear on the sender's statement until, say, 6 April. The sender would regard the payment as being made on 29 March and its cash book balance as reflecting the true position at that date.

Outstanding deposits/lodgements

In a similar way, a trader may receive cheques by post on 31 March, enter them in the cash book and pay them into the bank on the same day. Nevertheless, the cheques may not appear on the bank statement until 2 April. Again the cash book would be regarded as showing the true position. Outstanding deposits are also known as outstanding lodgements.

Proforma bank reconciliation
Cash book

Bal b/f	X	Bal b/f	X
Adjustments	X	Adjustments	X
Revised bal c/f	X	Revised bal c/f	X
	——		——
	X		X
	——		——
Revised bal b/f	X	Revised bal b/f	X

Bank reconciliation statement as at …..

	$
Balance per bank statement	X
Outstanding cheques	(X)
Outstanding lodgements	X
Other adjustments to the bank statement	X/(X)
	——
Balance per cash book (revised)	X

- Beware of overdrawn balances on the bank statement.
- Beware of debits/credits to bank statements.
- Beware of aggregation of deposits in a bank statement.
- Note that the bank balance on the statement of financial position is always the balance per the revised cash book.

CONTROL ACCOUNTS

Introduction

Control accounts are general ledger accounts that summarise a large number of transactions. As such they are part of the double entry system. They are used to prove the accuracy of the ledger accounting system. They are mainly used with regard to receivables and payables balances.

Accounting entries for credit sales and purchases

When a company transfers the daily total of the sales book into the general ledger the double entry is:

Dr Receivables ledger control account
Cr Sales revenue.

When they transfer the total of the purchase day book the double entry is:

Dr Purchases
Cr Payables ledger control account

Memorandum accounts

Whilst maintaining control accounts most businesses will maintain what is referred to as a 'memorandum.' This is a separate list of individual receivable and payable amounts due from each customer and to each supplier, respectively. This simple 'list of balances' is used as a record so that companies know how much each customer is due to pay and how much they are due to pay each supplier. This assists with credit control and cash flow management.

A key control operated by a business is to compare the total balance on the control account at the end of the accounting period with the total of all the separate memorandum balances. In theory they should be identical. This is referred to as control account reconciliation.

Note: the memorandum balances are often, confusingly, referred to as the 'receivables ledger' and the 'payables ledger.' Don't get these mixed up with the control accounts in the main/general ledger!

ILLUSTRATIVE CONTROL ACCOUNTS

Receivables ledger control account

Balance b/f	X	Balance b/f	X
Credit sales (SDB)	X	Sales returns (SRDB)	X
		Bank (CB)	X
Bank (CB) dishonoured cheques	X	Irrecoverable debts (journal)	X
Bank (CB) refunds of credit balances	X	Discounts allowed	X
Interest charged	X	Contra	X
Balance c/f	X	Balance c/f	X
	X		X
Balance b/f	X	Balance b/f	X

Payables ledger control account

Balance b/f	X	Balance b/f	X
Bank (CB)	X	Credit purchases (PDB)	X
Purchases returns (PRDB)	X	Bank (CB) refunds of debit balances	X
Discounts received	X		
Contra	X		
Balance c/f	X	Balance c/f	X
	X		X
Balance b/f	X	Balance b/f	X

Abbreviation key:
SDB Sales day book
PDB Purchases day book
SRDB Sales returns day book
PRDB Purchases returns day book
CB Cash book

Note that any entries to the control accounts must also be reflected in the individual memorandum accounts.

CONTRA ENTRIES

The situation may arise where a customer is also a supplier. Instead of both owing each other money, it may be agreed that the balances are contra's, i.e. cancelled.

The double entry for this type of contra is:

Dr Payables ledger control account

Cr Receivables ledger control account

The individual receivable and payable memorandum accounts must also be updated to reflect this.

Credit/debit balances in the wrong account

Sometimes the receivables ledger control account may show a credit balance, i.e. we owe the customer money. These amounts are usually small and arise when:

- The customer has overpaid.
- Credit notes have been issued for fully-paid-for goods.
- Payment is received in advance of raising invoices.

The payables ledger control account may show a debit balance for similar reasons.

Technically such balances should not exist and should be transferred to the correct account.

Thus a credit in a receivable account should be adjusted as follows:

Dr Receivables

Cr Payables

Debit balances in the payables ledger will be adjust using exactly the same double entry.

CONTROL ACCOUNT RECONCILIATIONS

Introduction

The reconciliation is a working to ensure that the entries in the sales and purchase ledgers (the memorandums, or list of individual balances) agree with the entries in the control accounts. The totals in each should be exactly the same. If not it indicates an error in either the memorandum account or the control account. All discrepancies should be investigated and corrected.

Preparing a control account reconciliation

The format of control account reconciliation, in this case for receivables, is as follows:

Receivables ledger control account			
	$		$
Balance given by the examiner	X	Adjustments for errors	X
Adjustments for errors	X	Revised balance c/f	X
	—		—
	X		X

Reconciliation of individual receivables balances with control account balance

	$
Balance as extracted from list of receivables	X
Adjustments for errors	X/(X)
	—
Revised total agreeing with balance c/f on control account	X

Illustration – Preparing a control account reconciliation

Alston's payables ledger control account is an integral part of the double entry system. Individual ledger account balances are listed and totalled on a monthly basis, and reconciled to the control account balance. Information for the month of March is as follows:

(1) Individual ledger account balances at 31 March have been listed out and totalled $19,766.

(2) The payables ledger control account balance at 31 March is $21,832.

(3) On further examination the following errors are discovered:

- The total of discount received for the month, amounting to $1,715, has not been entered in the control account but has been entered in the individual ledger accounts.
- On listing-out, an individual credit balance of $205 has been incorrectly treated as a debit.
- A petty cash payment to a supplier amounting to $63 has been correctly treated in the control account, but no entry has been made in the supplier's individual ledger account.
- The purchases day book total for March has been under cast (understated) by $2,000.

- Contras (set-offs) with the receivables ledger, amounting in total to $2,004, have been correctly treated in the individual ledger accounts but no entry has been made in the control account.

Step 1

The total of discount received in the cash book should have been debited to the payables ledger control account and credited to discount received. Thus, if the posting has not been entered in either double entry account it clearly should be. As this has already been entered into the individual ledger accounts, no adjustment is required to the list of balances.

Step 2

Individual credit balances are extracted from the payables ledger. Here, this error affects the ledger accounts balance. No adjustment is required to the control account, only to the list of balances.

Step 3

The information clearly states that the error has been made in the individual ledger accounts. Amendments should be made to the list of balances. Again, no amendment is required to the control accounts.

Step 4

The total of the purchases day book is posted by debiting purchases and crediting payables ledger control account. If the total is understated, the following bookkeeping entry must be made, posting the $2,000 understatement:

Dr Purchases

Cr Payables ledger control account

As the individual ledger accounts in the payables ledger are posted individually from the purchases day book, the total of the day book being understated will not affect the listing of the balances in the payables ledger.

Step 5

Here it is clear that the error affects the control account, not the payables ledger. Correction should be made by the bookkeeping entry:

Dr Payables ledger control account

Cr Receivables ledger control account

Payables ledger control account

20X9	$	20X9	$
Discount received	1,715	31 Mar	
Sales receivable ledger control	2,004	Balance	21,832
Balance c/f	20,113	Purchase	2,000
	———		———
	23,832		23,832

Reconciliation of individual balances with control account balance

	Cr
	$
Balances as extracted	19,766
Credit balance incorrectly treated 2 x $205	410
Petty cash payment	(63)
	———
Net total agreeing with control account	20,113

PREPARING BASIC FINANCIAL STATEMENTS
The process of preparing financial statements
The basic financial reporting process is as follows:

- transactions and events are recorded in the books of prime entry,
- totals from the books of prime entry are entered into the general ledger accounts,
- the control accounts are reconciled,
- the ledgers are balanced off,
- a trial balance is produced,
- errors are corrected,
- year-end journals are made,
- the financial statements are extracted from the final, extended trial balance.

Year-end adjustments to the initial trial balance
As well as adjusting the trial balance figures for any errors identified there are also a number of common adjustments made at the end of the accounting period. These include:

- closing inventory
- depreciation for the year
- accruals and prepayments
- irrecoverable debts and allowances for doubtful debts
- income tax
- provisions and contingent liabilities, and
- events after the reporting period

These adjustments need to be processed before the financial statements can be created.

Common year-end adjustments
The following is a list of some of the common year-end adjustments that would be made prior to preparing the financial statements:
(i) Closing inventory
Dr Inventory (SFP)
Cr Cost of sales (IS)

(ii) Depreciation charge for the year
Dr Depreciation expense (IS)
Cr Accumulated depreciation (SFP)

(iii) Accruals (chapter 10)
Dr Expenses (IS)
Cr Accrual (Liability) (SFP)

(iv) Prepayments
Dr Prepayment (Current Asset) (SFP)
Cr Expenses (IS)

(v) Irrecoverable debts
Dr Irrecoverable debt expense (IS)
Cr Receivables (SFP)

(vi) Allowance for receivables
Increase in allowance:
Dr Irrecoverable debt expense (IS)
Cr Allowance for receivables (SFP)
Decrease in allowance:
Dr Allowance for receivables (SFP)
Cr Irrecoverable debt expense (IS)

(vii) Tax estimate for the year
Dr Tax charge (IS)
Cr Current tax liabilities (SFP)

(viii) Adjustments for prior year tax estimates
Overprovision in prior year:
Dr Current tax provision (SFP)
Cr Tax charge for the year (IS)
Underprovision in prior year:
Dr Tax charge for the year (IS)
Cr Current tax provision (SFP)

IAS 1 PRESENTATION OF FINANCIAL STATEMENTS

The required formats for published company financial statements are provided by IAS1. This requires the following components to be presented:

- a statement of financial position
- an income statement
- a statement of comprehensive income
- a statement of changes in equity
- a statement of cash flows, and
- notes to the accounts.

THE STATEMENT OF CASH FLOWS

The difference between profit and cash

Whilst a business might be profitable this does not mean they will be able to survive. To achieve this they need cash to be able to pay their debts. If they could not pay their debts they would be put into administration or liquidated.

The main reason for this problem is that profit is not the same as cash flow. Profits (from the income statement) are calculated on the accruals basis. Most goods and services are sold on credit so at the point of sale revenue is recognised but no cash is received. The same can be said of credit purchases. There are also a number of expenses that are recognised that have no cash impact; depreciation is a good example of this. So a business can at the same time be profitable but have no cash left to pay its suppliers.

For this reason it is important that users of the financial statements can assess the cash position of a business at the end of the year but also how cash has been used and generated by the business during the accounting period.

Cash flow management

As mentioned above, cash flow is vital to the survival of a company both in the long and the short term. To reflect this, one of the key measures of the health of a business is solvency or liquidity.

In summary management have various liquid assets at their disposal that they can use to settle their debts in the short term. These include inventory, receivables and cash (i.e. current assets). They are used to pay off overdrafts, trade payables, loan interest and tax balances (i.e. current liabilities).

Management should maintain sufficient current assets to be able to pay their current liabilities as they fall due. If they do not, they will default their payments, lose supplier goodwill or suffer fines and sanctions. In the worst case scenario a supplier, lender or tax authority may even have a company put into administration or liquidation in an attempt to recover amounts due to them.

To ensure an effective balance management must consider inventory production and storage cycles and have an effective system of credit control to ensure cash is received into the business as soon as possible. On the flip side they must also manage the level of debt they expose the business to.

IAS 7 STATEMENT OF CASH FLOWS

The objectives of IAS 7 are to ensure that companies:

- report their cash generation and cash absorption for a period by highlighting the significant components of cash flow in a way that facilitates comparison of the cash flow performance of different businesses.
- provide information that assists in the assessment of their liquidity, solvency and financial adaptability.

FORMAT OF A STATEMENT OF CASH FLOWS

IAS 7 Statement of Cash Flows requires companies to prepare a statement of cash flows as part of their annual financial statements. The cash flow must be presented using standard headings. Note: there are two methods of reconciling cash from operating activities, the direct and indirect method.

Statement of cash flows for the period ended 31 December XXX		
	$000	$000
Cash flows from operating activities		
Cash generated from operations	X	
Interest paid	(X)	
Dividends paid	(X)	
Income taxes paid	(X)	
	_____	
Net cash from operating activities		X
Cash flows from investing activities		
Purchase of property, plant and equipment	(X)	
Proceeds of sale of equipment	X	
Interest received	X	
Dividends received	X	
	_____	
Net cash used in investing activities		(X)
Cash flows from financing activities		
Proceeds of issue of shares	X	
Repayment of loans	(X)	
Dividends paid	–	
	_____	
Net cash used in financing activities		(X)
		_____
Net increase in cash and cash equivalents		X

Cash and cash equivalents at the beginning of the period	X
	———
Cash and cash equivalents at the end of the period	X
	———

Cash generated from operations

There are two methods of calculating cash from operations – the direct or indirect method. The method used will depend upon the information provided within the question.

Direct method

This method uses information contained in the ledger accounts of the company to calculate the cash from operations figure as follows:

	$	$
Cash sales		X
Cash received from receivables		X
		———
		X
Less:		
Cash purchases	X	
Cash paid to credit suppliers	X	
Cash expenses	X	
		(X)
	———	———
Cash generated from operations		X

Indirect method

This method reconciles between profit before tax (as reported in the income statement) and cash generated from operations as follows:

	$
Profit before tax	X
Finance cost	X
Investment income	(X)
Depreciation charge	X
Loss/(profit) on disposal of non-current assets	X/(X)
(Increase)/decrease in inventories	(X)/X
(Increase)/decrease in trade receivables	(X)/X
Increase/(decrease) in trade payables	X/(X)
	———
Cash generated from operations	X

This working begins with the profit before tax as shown in the income statement. The remaining figures are the adjustments necessary to convert the profit figure to the cash flow for the period.

Adjustments to profit before tax:

- Depreciation – Added back to profit because it is a non-cash expense
- Interest expense – Added back because it is not part of cash generated from operations (the interest actually paid is deducted later)
- Increase in trade receivables – Deducted because this is part of the profit not yet realised into cash but tied up in receivables
- Decrease in inventories – Added on because the decrease in inventories liberates extra cash
- Decrease in trade payables – Deducted because the reduction in payables must reduce cash

THE STATEMENT OF CHANGES IN EQUITY

- Overview
- Equity represents the owners' interests in the company. An alternative way of defining it is that it represents what is left in the business when it ceases to trade, all the assets are sold off and all the liabilities are paid. This can then be distributed to the equity holders (ordinary shareholders).
- It is made up primarily of share capital (including share premium) and reserves. The main reserves are the revaluation reserve and retained earnings.

Revaluation reserve

- This is created to recognise the gain made when non-current assets are revalued. The gain is not real so cannot be included in the profit reserves of the business. However, the gain would still form part of the value repaid to the equity holders if the business were sold off at that point in time.

Retained earnings

- This represents the sum total of all the profits and losses made by the business since its incorporation and that have not yet been paid to shareholders as a dividend.
- As these elements are particularly relevant to shareholders (it helps them value their wealth or 'share of the pie') it is important to ensure the shareholders understand any movements in these balances. For this reason a statement of changes in equity is required. It summarises the opening and closing positions on all these accounts and identifies the reason for the movements in between the two periods.

	Share capital $m	Share premium $m	Revaluation reserve $m	Retained earnings $m	Total $m
Balance at 1 January	X	X	X	X	X
Equity shares issued	X	X			X
Revaluation surplus			X		X
Net profit				X	X
Dividends				(X)	(X)
Bal at 31 Dec	X	X	X	X	X

Illustrative Statement of changes in equity for XYZ Ltd

THE STATEMENT OF COMPREHENSIVE INCOME

The Income Statement

This summarises the incomes earned and expenses incurred during the financial period.

XYZ Group

Income statement for the year ended 31 December 2014

	$
Revenue	X
Cost of sales	(X)
Gross profit	X
Distribution costs	(X)
Administrative expenses	(X)
Profit from operations	X
Investment income	X
Finance costs	(X)
Profit before tax	X
Tax expense	(X)
Net profit for the period	X

The statement of comprehensive income

This is simply an extension of the income statement. The reason for this is that some gains the business makes during the year are not realised gains. The main example is the revaluation of tangible assets. The gain is not realised until the asset is sold and converted into cash. The revaluation represents a hypothetical gain (i.e. what gain would a company make if the asset was sold).

For this reason it should not be included in net profit for the period, which represents the profit earned from realised sales. Instead the unrealised gains are added onto the end of the income statement, as follows:

Statement of comprehensive income for XYZ for the year ended 31 December 2014

	$m
Revenue	X
Cost of sales	(X)
Gross profit	X
Distribution costs	(X)
Administrative expenses	(X)
Profit from operations	X
Investment income	X
Finance costs	(X)
Profit before tax	X
Tax expense	(X)
Net profit for the period	X
Other comprehensive income:	
Gain/loss on property revaluation	X/(X)
Total comprehensive income for the year	**X**

Items requiring separate disclosure
Certain items need to be separately disclosed on the face of the income statement so that they are clearly visible to the users of the financial statements. The main items requiring such treatment are significant, one-off transactions or events. They need to be disclosed because they are not part of the normal trading activity of the business and could significantly distort the reported profits or losses for the year. They include:
- restructuring or reorganisation of the company
- profits or losses on disposal of property, plant and equipment (or investments), and
- impairments of inventory, property, plant and equipment.

All such items should be included on their own, separate line in the income statement/statement of comprehensive income.

The Statement of Financial Position
This summarises the asset, liability and equity balances (i.e. the financial position of the company) at the end of the accounting period.

Illustrative statement of financial position for XYZ at 31 December XXXX

	$m	$m
Non-current assets		
Property, plant and equipment	X	
Investments	X	
Intangibles	X	
	────	
		X
Current assets		
Inventories	X	
Trade and other receivables	X	
Prepayments	X	
Cash	X	
	────	
		X
		────
Total assets		**X**
		────
Equity		
Ordinary share capital	X	
Irredeemable preference share capital	X	
Share premium	X	
Reserves:	────	
Retained earnings	X	
	────	
		X
Non-current liabilities		
Loan notes		X
Current liabilities		
Trade and other payables	X	
Overdrafts	X	
Tax payable	X	
	────	
		X
		────
Total equity and liabilities		**X**
		────

Current assets and current liabilities
The suggested statement of financial position format makes a distinction between current and non-current assets and liabilities. IAS 1 sets down the rules to be applied in making this distinction.

Assets
An asset should be classified as a current asset if it is:
- held primarily for trading purposes
- expected to be realised within 12 months of the statement of financial position date; or
- cash or a cash equivalent (i.e. a short term investment, such as a 30 day bond).

All other assets should be classified as non-current assets.

Note that this definition allows inventory or receivables to qualify as current assets under (a) above, even if they may not be realised into cash within twelve months.

Liabilities
The rules for current liabilities are similar to those for current assets.

A liability should be classified as a current liability if:
- it is expected to be settled in the normal course of the enterprise's operating cycle
- it is held primarily for the purpose of being traded
- it is due to be settled within 12 months of the statement of financial position date or
- the company does not have an unconditional right to defer settlement for at least 12 months after the statement of financial position date.

All other liabilities should be classified as non-current liabilities.

THE TRIAL BALANCE AND ERRORS IN THE FINANCIAL REPORTING SYSTEM
The Trial Balance
At the end of the year, once all ledger accounts have been balanced off, the closing balances are summarised on a long list of balances. This is referred to as a trial balance.

All the closing debit balances are summarised in one column and the closing credit balances in another. Given the nature of the double entry system the totals of both columns should agree. If not the discrepancy must be investigated and corrected.

This is another control in the accounting system to ensure that the balances reported in the financial statements are accurate. The layout of a trial balance is illustrated below:

Trial Balance as at 31 December 20X5

	Dr	Cr
	$	$
Revenue		X
Purchases	X	
Administrative expenses	X	
Non-current assets	X	
Trade receivables	X	

Cash	X	
Share capital		X
Loans		X
Trade payables		X
	___	___
	X	X

The figures reported on the final trial balance will be transferred to the financial statements. It is therefore vital to adjust the trial balance for any identified errors.

TYPE OF ERROR

Errors where the trial balance still balances

- **Error of omission:** A transaction has been completely omitted from the accounting records, e.g. a cash sale of $100 was not recorded.
- **Error of commission**: A transaction has been recorded in the wrong account, e.g. rates expense of $500 has been debited to the rent account in error.
- **Error of principle:** A transaction has conceptually been recorded incorrectly, e.g. a non-current asset purchase of $1,000 has been debited to the repair expense account rather than an asset account.
- **Compensating error:** Two different errors have been made which cancel each other out, e.g. a rent bill of $1,200 has been debited to the rent account as $1,400 and a casting error on the sales account has resulted in sales being overstated by $200.
- **Error of original entry:** The correct double entry has been made but with the wrong amount, e.g. a cash sale of $76 has been recorded as $67.
- **Reversal of entries:** The correct amount has been posted to the correct accounts but on the wrong side, e.g. a cash sale of $200 has been debited to sales and credited to bank.

Errors where the trial balance does not balance

- Single sided entry – a debit entry has been made but no corresponding credit entry or vice versa.
- Debit and credit entries have been made but at different values.
- Two debit or two credit entries have been posted.
- An incorrect addition in any individual account, i.e. miscasting.
- Opening balance has not been brought down.
- Extraction error – the balance in the trial balance is different from the balance in the relevant account or the balance from the ledger account has been placed in the wrong column of the TB.

If there is a difference on the trial balance, then a suspense account is used to make the total debits equal the total credits:

	$	$
Non-current assets	5,000	
Receivables	550	
Inventory	1,000	
Cash	200	

Payables		600
Loan		2,000
Share capital		4,000
Suspense account		150
	———	———
	6,750	6,750

The balance on the suspense account must be cleared before final accounts can be prepared. Corrections to any of the six errors mentioned above will affect the suspense account.

Suspense accounts

A suspense account is an account in which debits or credits are held temporarily until sufficient information is available for them to be posted to the correct accounts.

There are two main reasons why suspense accounts may be created:

- On the extraction of a trial balance the debits are not equal to the credits and the difference is put to a suspense account.
- When a bookkeeper performing double entry is not sure where to post one side of an entry he may debit or credit a suspense account and leave the entry there until its ultimate destination is clarified.

Correction of errors

When correcting errors it is useful to think about:

- What double entry should have been made:
- What double entry was made?
- What is the correcting journal?

For example: the purchase of a non-current asset costing $100 has been recorded by debiting $10 to the non-current assets account and crediting $100 to cash.

What should the double entry have been?		What was the double entry?		Correcting journal	
Dr NCA	$100	Dr NCA	$10	Dr NCA	$90
Cr Cash	$100	Dr Suspense (bal. fig)	$90	Cr Suspense	$90
		Cr Cash	$100		

Adjustments to profit

The correction journal may result in a change in profit, depending on whether the journal debits or credits the income statement:

Dr Statement of financial position account Cr Statement of financial position account	No impact on profit
Dr Income statement account Cr Income statement account	No impact on profit
Dr Income statement account Cr Statement of financial position account	Profit decreases
Dr Statement of financial position account Cr Income statement account	Profit increases

CHAPTER THREE
THE CONTEXT AND PURPOSE OF FINANCIAL REPORTING

Overview

Financial reporting plays a vital role in world economies. Its primary purpose is to provide relevant and useful information to the owners of a company where there is a division between the ownership and control of that company. This occurs mainly in public limited companies, where share capital is sold to the public through a stock market/exchange system. The diverse and potentially geographically dispersed shareholders do not get involved in the management of their company; they appoint directors to do this on their behalf. The owners receive an annual statement summarising the performance and position of their company so that they can assess how well their investment has performed during the reporting period.

Without this reporting system investors would be less inclined to part with their capital as they would have no way of monitoring how effectively the company is being run by the directors, the appointed stewards of the company who are supposed to be operating in the best interests of the shareholders.

In order to meet the needs of the users of the financial statements companies have to implement accounting systems that provide the information needed. It is also important that this system is regulated to ensure that the information provided to the users is in an appropriate format and that it is useful to their informational requirements. This is achieved through a financial reporting framework, the basis of which is a conceptual framework.

ACCOUNTING

Overview

The accounting system of a business records and summarises the financial performance/position of a business over/at a certain period of time. This information is crucial to various stakeholders of the business, who will analyse that information to make significant economic decisions. It is of vital importance that these stakeholders have good quality information to be able to make good quality decisions.

FINANCIAL AND MANAGEMENT ACCOUNTING

Financial accounting

Financial accounting is concerned with the production of financial statements for external users. Financial statements report on the directors' stewardship of the funds entrusted to them by the shareholders.

Investors need to be able to choose which companies to invest in and compare their investments. In order to facilitate comparison, financial accounts are prepared using accepted accounting conventions and standards. International Accounting Standards (IASs) and International Financial Reporting Standards (IFRSs) help to reduce the differences in the way that companies draw up their financial statements in different countries.

The financial statements are public documents, and therefore they will not reveal details about, for example, individual products' profitability.

MANAGEMENT ACCOUNTING

Management require much more detailed and up-to-date information in order to control the business and plan for the future. They need to be able to cost-out products and production methods, assess profitability and so on. In order to facilitate this, management accounts present information in any way which may be useful to management, for example by operating unit or product line.

Management accounting is an integral part of management activity concerned with identifying, presenting and interpreting information used for:

- formulating strategy
- planning and controlling activities
- decision making
- optimising the use of resources.

FINANCIAL STATEMENTS

The financial statements are the documents that are provided to the users to help them understand the financial position and performance of the reporting entity.

The components of financial statements

A set of financial statements include:

The statement of financial position

This summarises the assets, liabilities and equity balances of the business at the end of the reporting period. This used to be referred to as a 'balance sheet.'

The statement of comprehensive income

This summarises the revenues earned and expenses incurred by the business throughout the whole of the reporting period. This used to be referred to as a 'profit and loss account.'

The statement of changes in equity

This summarises the movement in equity balances (share capital, share premium, revaluation reserve and retained earnings) from the beginning of the reporting period to the end.

The statement of cash flows

This summarises the cash physically paid and received throughout the reporting period.

The notes

These comprise the accounting policies disclosures and any other disclosures required to enable to the shareholders to make informed decisions about the business.

THE CONCEPTUAL FRAMEWORK

The Conceptual Framework for Financial Reporting 2010 underpins the preparation of financial statements. It presents the main ideas, concepts and principles upon which all International Financial Reporting Standards, and therefore financial statements, are based. It includes discussion of:

- the objectives of financial reporting

- the qualitative characteristics of useful financial information
- the definition, recognition and measurement of the elements from which the financial statements are constructed
- the accruals and going concern concepts, and
- the concepts of capital and capital maintenance.

Framework Update

At present there is a long-term joint project in operation to update the the Framework. This will create a foundation for the development of future accounting standards that are principles based, internally consistent and internationally converged. Ultimately, it will replace the Framework for the Preparation and Presentation of Financial Statements which was first published in 1989. As this project progresses and individual chapters are approved, the new Conceptual Framework for Financial Reporting 2010 will be updated and the superseded provisions of the original Framework document will be deleted.

Phase A, which updated the objectives and qualitative characteristics of financial statements, was approved in September 2010. There are no significant changes to the underlying purposes and objectives of the Framework as established in the 1989. There has, however, been an update to the qualitative characteristics of financial statements

CHAPTER FOUR
INTERNATIONAL FINANCIAL REPORTING STANDARDS

Harmonisation

Due to the increasingly global nature of investment and business operation there has been a move towards the 'internationalisation' of financial reporting. This 'harmonisation' was considered necessary to provide consistent and comparable information to an increasingly global audience.

If companies use different methods of accounting then before any decisions can be made about different entities the accounts would have to be re-written so that the accounting concepts and principles applied are the same; only then relevant comparisons be made.

Legal stature

IFRS's are not enforceable in any country; they are developed by an international organisation that has no international authority. To become enforceable they must be adopted by a country's national financial reporting standard setter.

Within the European Union IFRS were adopted for all listed entities in 2005. Other countries to have adopted IFRS include; Argentina, Australia, Brazil, Canada, Russia, Mexico, Saudi Arabia and South Africa. The US, China and India are going through a process of 'convergence,' whereby they are updating their national standards over time so that they are consistent with IFRS.

IAS 1 PRESENTATION OF FINANCIAL STATEMENTS

Introduction

This standard prescribes the basis for presentation of general purpose financial statements to ensure comparability both with the entity's financial statements of previous periods and with the financial statements of other entities. It sets out overall requirements for the presentation of financial statements, guidelines for their structure and minimum requirements for their content.

Contents of the financial statements

A complete set of financial statements comprises:

- a statement of financial position as at the end of the period,
- a statement of comprehensive income for the period,
- a statement of changes in equity for the period,
- a statement of cash flows for the period, and
- notes, comprising a summary of significant accounting policies and other explanatory information.

Going concern

When preparing financial statements, management shall make an assessment of an entity's ability to continue as a going concern. An entity shall prepare financial statements on a going concern basis unless management either intends to liquidate the entity or to cease trading, or has no realistic alternative but to do so.

When management is aware of material uncertainties related to events or conditions that may cast significant doubt upon the entity's ability to continue as a going concern, the entity shall disclose those uncertainties in the financial statements.

Aggregation

An entity shall present separately each material class of similar items, i.e. all sales can be reported under the heading 'turnover'. An entity shall present separately items of a dissimilar nature or function unless they are immaterial.

Offsetting

An entity shall not offset assets and liabilities or income and expenses, unless required or permitted by an IFRS.

Comparatives

Except when IFRSs permit or require otherwise, an entity shall disclose comparative information in respect of the previous period for all amounts reported in the current period's financial statements. An entity shall include comparative information for narrative and descriptive information when it is relevant to an understanding of the current period's financial statements.

Notes

The notes shall:
- present information about the basis of preparation of the financial statements and the specific accounting policies used,
- disclose the information required by IFRSs that is not presented elsewhere in the financial statements, and
- provide information that is not presented elsewhere in the financial statements, but is relevant to an understanding of them.

Assumptions/judgements

An entity shall disclose, in the summary of significant accounting policies or other notes, the judgements that management has made in the process of applying the entity's accounting policies and that have the most significant effect on the amounts recognised in the financial statements.

An entity shall disclose information about the assumptions it makes about the future, and other major sources of estimation uncertainty at the end of the reporting period, that have a significant risk of resulting in a material adjustment to the carrying amounts of assets and liabilities within the next financial year.

IAS 2 INVENTORIES

Objective

The objective of this standard is to prescribe the accounting treatment for inventories. A particular focus is the cost to be recognised for closing inventories. The standard provides guidance on the determination of cost and its subsequent recognition as an expense, including any write-down to net realisable value.

Valuation of Inventory

Inventories shall be measured at the lower of cost and net realisable value.

Net realisable value is the estimated selling price in the ordinary course of business less the estimated costs of completion and the estimated costs necessary to make the sale.

The Cost of Inventory

The cost of inventories shall comprise all costs of purchase, costs of conversion and other costs incurred in bringing the inventories to their present location and condition.

The cost of inventories shall be assigned by using the first-in, first-out (FIFO) or weighted average cost formula. An entity shall use the same cost formula for all inventories having a similar nature and use to the entity. For inventories with a different nature or use, different cost formulas may be justified.

The Matching Principle

When inventories are sold, the carrying amount of those inventories shall be recognised as an expense in the period in which the related revenue is recognised.

The amount of any write-down of inventories to net realisable value and all losses of inventories shall be recognised as an expense in the period the write-down or loss occurs.

IAS 7 STATEMENT OF CASH FLOWS

Objective

The objective of this standard is to require the provision of information about the changes in cash and cash equivalents of a business by means of a statement of cash flows. This classifies cash flows during the period from operating, investing and financing activities.

Definition

Cash flows are inflows and outflows of cash and cash equivalents. Cash comprises cash on hand and demand deposits. Cash equivalents are short-term, highly liquid investments that are readily convertible to known amounts of cash and which are subject to an insignificant risk of changes in value.

Operating activities

Operating activities are the principal revenue-producing activities of the entity and other activities that are not investing or financing activities. Cash flows from operating activities are primarily derived from the principal revenue-producing activities of the entity, i.e. the sales that the business was primarily set up to make.

The amount of cash flows arising from operating activities is a key indicator of the extent to which the operations of the entity have generated sufficient cash flows to repay loans, maintain the operating capability of the entity, pay dividends and make new investments without needing external sources of financing.

An entity shall report cash flows from operating activities using either:

(a) the direct method, whereby major classes of gross cash receipts and gross cash payments are disclosed; or

(b) the indirect method, whereby profit or loss is adjusted for the effects of transactions of a non-cash nature and movements in inventory, receivables and payables.

Investing activities

Investing activities are the acquisition and disposal of long-term assets and other investments not included in cash equivalents. The disclosure of cash flows arising from investing activities is important because the cash flows represent the expenditure in resources intended to generate future income and cash flows.

Financing activities

Financing activities are activities that result in changes in the size and composition of the contributed equity and borrowings of the entity. The separate disclosure of cash flows arising from financing activities is important because it is useful in predicting the costs of servicing those sources of finance in the future.

IAS 8 ACCOUNTING POLICIES, CHANGES IN ACCOUNTING ESTIMATES AND ERRORS

Objective

The objective of this standard is to prescribe the criteria for selecting and changing accounting policies, together with the accounting treatment and disclosure of changes in accounting policies, changes in accounting estimates and corrections of errors. The standard is intended to enhance the relevance and reliability of an entity's financial statements, and the comparability of those financial statements over time and with the financial statements of other entities.

Accounting policies

Accounting policies are the specific principles, bases, conventions, rules and practices applied by an entity in preparing and presenting financial statements. When an IFRS specifically applies to a transaction, other event or condition, the accounting policy or policies applied to that item shall be determined by applying the IFRS and considering any relevant Implementation Guidance issued by the IASB for the IFRS.

In the absence of a standard or an Interpretation that specifically applies to a transaction, other event or condition, management shall use its judgement in developing and applying an accounting policy that results in information that is relevant and reliable. In making the judgement management shall refer to, and consider the applicability of, the following sources in descending order:

- the requirements and guidance in IFRSs dealing with similar and related issues; and
- the definitions, recognition criteria and measurement concepts for assets, liabilities, income and expenses in the Conceptual Framework.

Changes in accounting policy
An entity shall select and apply its accounting policies consistently for similar transactions, other events and conditions. An entity shall change an accounting policy only if the change:
- is required by an IFRS; or
- results in the financial statements providing reliable and more relevant information about the effects of transactions, other events or conditions on the entity's financial position, financial performance or cash flows.

An entity shall account for a change in accounting policy resulting from the initial application of an IFRS in
accordance with the specific transitional provisions, if any, in that IFRS. In general, a change in accounting policy shall be applied retrospectively, i.e. it should be applied to prior periods as though that policy had always been in place. This will require adjustment of the opening balances in the current year's accounts as well as adjustment of comparative balances.

Changes in accounting estimate
The use of reasonable estimates is an essential part of the preparation of financial statements and does not undermine their reliability. Changes in accounting estimates result from new information or new developments and, accordingly, are not corrections of errors. The effect of a change in an accounting estimate, shall be recognised prospectively by including it in profit or loss in:
- the period of the change, if the change affects that period only; or
- the period of the change and future periods, if the change affects both.

Prior period errors
Prior period errors are omissions from, and misstatements in, the entity's financial statements for one or more prior periods arising from a failure to use, or misuse of, reliable information that:
- was available when financial statements for those periods were authorised for issue; and
- could reasonably be expected to have been obtained and taken into account in the preparation and presentation of those financial statements.

Such errors include the effects of mathematical mistakes, mistakes in applying accounting policies, oversights or misinterpretations of facts, and fraud. An entity shall correct material prior period errors retrospectively in the first set of financial statements authorised for issue after their discovery by:
- restating the comparative amounts for the prior period(s) presented in which the error occurred; or
- if the error occurred before the earliest prior period presented, restating the opening balances of assets, liabilities and equity for the earliest prior period presented.

Materiality
Omissions or misstatements of items are material if they could, individually or collectively, influence the economic decisions of users taken on the basis of the financial statements. Materiality depends on the size and nature of the omission or misstatement judged in the

surrounding circumstances. The size or nature of the item, or a combination of both, could be the determining factor.

IAS 10 EVENTS AFTER THE REPORTING PERIOD

Objective

The objective of this standard is to prescribe:

- when an entity should adjust its financial statements for events after the reporting period; and
- the disclosures that an entity should give about the date when the financial statements were authorised for issue and about events after the reporting period.

The Standard also requires that an entity should not prepare its financial statements on a going concern basis if events after the reporting period indicate that the going concern assumption is not appropriate.

Definition

Events after the reporting period are those events, favourable and unfavourable, that occur between the end of the reporting period and the date when the financial statements are authorised for issue. Two types of events can be identified:

- those that provide evidence of conditions that existed at the end of the reporting period (adjusting events after the reporting period); and
- those that are indicative of conditions that arose after the reporting period (non-adjusting events after the reporting period).

Accounting treatment

An entity shall adjust the amounts recognised in its financial statements to reflect adjusting events after the reporting period. An entity shall not adjust the amounts recognised in its financial statements to reflect non-adjusting events after the reporting period.

If, however, non-adjusting events after the reporting period are material, non-disclosure could influence the economic decisions of users taken on the basis of the financial statements. Accordingly, an entity shall disclose the following for each material category of non-adjusting event after the reporting period:

- the nature of the event; and
- an estimate of its financial effect, or a statement that such an estimate cannot be made.

IAS 16 PROPERTIES, PLANT AND EQUIPMENT

Objective

The objective of this standard is to prescribe the accounting treatment for property, plant and equipment so that users of the financial statements can discern information about an entity's investment in its property, plant and equipment and the changes in such investments. The principal issues in accounting for property, plant and equipment are the recognition of the assets, the determination of their carrying amounts and the depreciation charges and impairment losses to be recognised in relation to them.

Definition
Property, plant and equipment are tangible items that:
- are held for use in the production or supply of goods or services, for rental to others, or for administrative purposes; and
- are expected to be used during more than one period.

Recognition
The cost of an item of property, plant and equipment shall be recognised as an asset if, and only if:
- it is probable that future economic benefits associated with the item will flow to the entity; and
- the cost of the item can be measured reliably.

Initial recognition
Property, plant and equipment shall be measured at its cost. The cost of an item of property, plant and equipment is the cash price equivalent at the recognition date. The cost of an item of property, plant and equipment comprises:
- its purchase price, including duties and non-refundable purchase taxes, after deducting trade
  discounts,
- any costs directly attributable to bringing the asset to the location and condition necessary for it to be capable of operating in the manner intended by management, and
- the initial estimate of the costs of dismantling and removing the item and restoring the site on which it is located, the obligation for which an entity incurs either when the item is acquired.

Subsequent measurement
An entity shall choose either the cost model or the revaluation model as its accounting policy and shall apply that policy to an entire class of property, plant and equipment.

Cost model
After recognition as an asset, an item of property, plant and equipment shall be carried at its cost less any accumulated depreciation and any accumulated impairment losses.

Revaluation model
After recognition as an asset, an item of property, plant and equipment whose fair value can be measured reliably shall be carried at a revalued amount, being its fair value at the date of the revaluation less any subsequent accumulated depreciation and subsequent accumulated impairment losses.
Revaluations shall be made with sufficient regularity to ensure that the carrying amount does not differ materially from that which would be determined using fair value at the end of the reporting period.

If an asset's carrying amount is increased as a result of a revaluation, the increase shall be recognised in other comprehensive income and accumulated in equity under the heading of revaluation surplus. The increase should only be recognised in profit or loss to the extent that it reverses a revaluation decrease of the same asset previously recognised in profit or loss. If an asset's carrying amount is decreased as a result of a revaluation, the decrease shall be recognised in profit or loss. However, if that asset has previously been increased in value due to a revaluation then the decrease shall be recognised first against any credit balances existing in the revaluation reserve relating to that asset. Once this has been consumed any remaining loss must be recognised in profit or loss.

Depreciation

Depreciation is the systematic allocation of the depreciable amount of an asset over its useful life, i.e. spreading the cost of the asset over the period it will be used to generate benefit. Depreciable amount is the cost of an asset, less its residual value.

The depreciation charge for each period shall be recognised in profit or loss. The depreciation method used shall reflect the pattern in which the asset's future economic benefits are expected to be consumed by the entity.

The residual value of an asset is the estimated amount that an entity would obtain from disposal of the asset, after deducting the estimated costs of disposal, if the asset were at the end of its useful life.

IAS 18, REVENUE

Objective

The primary issue in accounting for revenue is determining when to recognise it. Revenue is recognised when it is probable that future economic benefits will flow to the entity and these benefits can be measured reliably. IAS 18 identifies the circumstances in which these criteria will be met and, therefore, revenue will be recognised.

Definition

Revenue is the gross inflow of economic benefits during the period arising in the course of the ordinary activities of an entity that result in increases in equity (other than increases relating to contributions from equity participants, i.e. selling more share capital).

Measurement

Revenue shall be measured at the fair value of the consideration received or receivable. Fair value is the amount for which an asset could be exchanged, or a liability settled, between knowledgeable, willing parties in an arm's length transaction. The amount of revenue arising on a transaction is usually determined by agreement between the entity and the buyer or user of the asset. It is measured at the fair value of the consideration received or receivable taking into account the amount of any trade discounts and volume rebates allowed by the entity.

Sale of goods
Revenue from the sale of goods shall be recognised when all the following conditions have been satisfied:
- the entity has transferred to the buyer the significant risks and rewards of ownership of the goods;
- the entity retains neither continuing managerial involvement associated with ownership nor effective control over the goods sold;
- the amount of revenue can be measured reliably;
- it is probable that the economic benefits associated with the transaction will flow to the entity; and
- the costs incurred or to be incurred in respect of the transaction can be measured reliably.

Provision of services
When the outcome of a transaction involving the provision of services can be estimated reliably, revenue associated with the transaction shall be recognised by reference to the stage of completion of the transaction at the end of the reporting period.
The outcome of a transaction can be estimated reliably when all the following conditions are satisfied:
- the amount of revenue can be measured reliably;
- it is probable that the economic benefits associated with the transaction will flow to the entity;
- the stage of completion of the transaction at the end of the reporting period can be measured reliably; and
- the costs incurred for the transaction and the costs to complete the transaction can be measured reliably.

The recognition of revenue by reference to the stage of completion of a transaction is often referred to as the percentage of completion method. Under this method, revenue is recognised in the accounting periods in which the services are rendered. The recognition of revenue on this basis provides useful information on the extent of service activity and performance during a period.
When the outcome of the transaction involving the rendering of services cannot be estimated reliably, revenue shall be recognised only to the extent of the expenses recognised that are recoverable (i.e. neither a profit nor a loss is recognised).

IAS 37 PROVISIONS, CONTINGENT LIABILITIES AND CONTINGENT ASSETS
Objective
The objective of IAS 37 is to ensure that appropriate recognition criteria and measurement bases are applied to provisions, contingent liabilities and contingent assets and that sufficient information is disclosed in the notes to enable users to understand their nature, timing and amount.

Provisions
A provision is a liability of uncertain timing or amount.

Recognition
A provision should be recognised when:
- an entity has a present obligation (legal or constructive) as a result of a past event;
- it is probable that an outflow of economic benefits will be required to settle the obligation; and
- a reliable estimate can be made of the amount of the obligation.

If these conditions are not met, no provision shall be recognised.

Measurement
The amount recognised as a provision shall be the best estimate of the expenditure required to settle the present obligation at the end of the reporting period. Where the provision being measured involves a large population of items, the obligation is estimated by weighting all possible outcomes by their associated probabilities. Where a single obligation is being measured,
the individual most likely outcome may be the best estimate of the liability. However, even in such a case, the entity considers other possible outcomes.

Contingent liabilities
A contingent liability is:
- a possible obligation that arises from past events and whose existence will be confirmed only by the occurrence or non-occurrence of one or more uncertain future events not wholly within the control of the entity; or
- a present obligation that arises from past events but is not recognised because it is not probable that an outflow of economic benefits will be required to settle the obligation; or
- a present obligation that arises from past events but is not recognised because the amount of the obligation cannot be measured with sufficient reliability.

Disclosure
Entities do not recognise contingent liabilities (i.e. they do not record an expense and a liability). An entity should disclose a contingent liability in a note, unless the possibility of an outflow of economic benefits is remote.

Contingent assets
A contingent asset is a possible asset that arises from past events and whose existence will be confirmed only by the occurrence or non-occurrence of one or more uncertain future events not wholly within the control of the entity.
An entity shall not recognise a contingent asset. When the realisation of income is virtually certain, then the related asset is not a contingent asset and its recognition as revenue is appropriate.

IAS 38 INTANGIBLE ASSETS

Objective
The objective of IAS 38 is to prescribe the accounting treatment for intangible assets that are not dealt with specifically in another Standard. It requires an entity to recognise an intangible asset if, and only if, specified criteria are met. The standard also specifies how to measure the carrying amount of intangible assets and requires specified disclosures about intangible assets.

Definition
An intangible asset is an identifiable non-monetary asset without physical substance.

Recognition
The recognition of an item as an intangible asset requires an entity to demonstrate that the item meets:
- the definition of an intangible asset; and
- the recognition criteria.

This requirement applies to costs incurred initially to acquire or internally generate an intangible asset and those incurred subsequently to add to, replace part of, or service it.
An asset is identifiable if it either:
- is separable, i.e. it is capable of being separated or divided from the entity and sold, transferred, licensed, rented or exchanged; or
- arises from contractual or other legal rights

An intangible asset shall be recognised if, and only if:
- it is probable that the expected future economic benefits that are attributable to the asset will flow to the entity; and
- the cost of the asset can be measured reliably.

Measurement
An intangible asset shall be measured initially at cost. The cost of a separately acquired intangible asset comprises:
- its purchase price, including duties and non-refundable purchase taxes, after deducting trade discounts and rebates; and
- any directly attributable cost of preparing the asset for its intended use.

Internally generated assets
Internally generated goodwill shall not be recognised as an asset.
Internally generated brands, mastheads, publishing titles, customer lists and items similar in substance shall not be recognised as intangible assets.

Research and development
Expenditure on research (or on the research phase of an internal project) shall be recognised as an expense when it is incurred.
An intangible asset arising from development (or from the development phase of an internal project) shall be recognised if, and only if, an entity can demonstrate all of the following:

- the technical feasibility of completing the intangible asset so that it will be available for use or sale.
- its intention to complete the intangible asset and use or sell it.
- its ability to use or sell the intangible asset.
- how the intangible asset will generate probable future economic benefits. Among other things, the entity can demonstrate the existence of a market for the output of the intangible asset or the intangible asset itself or, if it is to be used internally, the usefulness of the intangible asset.
- the availability of adequate technical, financial and other resources to complete the development and to use or sell the intangible asset.
- its ability to measure reliably the expenditure attributable to the intangible asset during its development.

Measurement after recognition

An entity shall choose either the cost model or the revaluation model as its accounting policy. If an intangible asset is accounted for using the revaluation model, all the other assets in its class shall also be accounted for using the same model, unless there is no active market for those assets.

Cost model

After initial recognition, an intangible asset shall be carried at its cost less any accumulated amortisation and any accumulated impairment losses.

Revaluation model

After initial recognition, an intangible asset shall be carried at a revalued amount, being its fair value at the date of the revaluation less any subsequent accumulated amortisation and any subsequent accumulated impairment losses.

For the purpose of revaluations under this standard, fair value shall be measured by reference to an active market. Revaluations shall be made with such regularity that at the end of the reporting period the carrying amount of the asset does not differ materially from its fair value. An active market is a market in which all the following conditions exist:

- the items traded in the market are homogeneous;
- willing buyers and sellers can normally be found at any time; and
- prices are available to the public.

Useful life

An entity shall assess whether the useful life of an intangible asset is finite or indefinite. An intangible asset shall be regarded by the entity as having an indefinite useful life when, based an an analysis of all of the relevant factors, there is no foreseeable limit to the period over which the asset is expected to generate net cash inflows for the entity.

The useful life of an intangible asset that arises from contractual or other legal rights shall not exceed the period of the contractual or other legal rights, but may be shorter depending on the period over which the entity expects to use the asset. If the contractual or other legal rights are conveyed for a limited term that can be renewed, the useful life of the intangible asset shall include the renewal period(s) only if there is evidence to support renewal by the entity without significant cost.

Intangible assets with finite useful lives

The depreciable amount of an intangible asset with a finite useful life shall be allocated on a systematic basis over its useful life.

Depreciable amount is the cost of an asset, or other amount substituted for cost, less its residual value. Amortisation shall begin when the asset is available for use, ie when it is in the location and condition necessary for it to be capable of operating in the manner intended by management.

The amortisation method used shall reflect the pattern in which the asset's future economic benefits are expected to be consumed by the entity. If that pattern cannot be determined reliably, the straight-line method shall be used. The amortisation charge for each period shall be recognised in profit or loss.

The residual value of an intangible asset is the estimated amount that an entity would obtain from disposal of the asset, after deducting the estimated costs of disposal, if the asset were at the end of its useful life.

The residual value of an intangible asset with a finite useful life shall be assumed to be zero unless:

- there is a commitment by a third party to purchase the asset at the end of its useful life; or
- there is an active market for the asset and residual value can be determined by reference to that market and it is probable that such a market will exist at the end of the asset's useful life.

Intangible assets with indefinite useful lives

An intangible asset with an indefinite useful life shall not be amortised. In accordance with IAS 36 Impairment of Assets, an entity is required to test an intangible asset with an indefinite useful life for impairment by comparing its recoverable amount with its carrying amount annually and whenever there is an indication that the intangible asset may be impaired.

The useful life of an intangible asset that is not being amortised shall be reviewed each period to determine whether events and circumstances continue to support an indefinite useful life assessment for that asset. If they do not, the change in the useful life assessment from indefinite to finite shall be accounted for as a change in an accounting estimate in accordance with IAS 8.

STRUCTURE OF THE IFRS REGULATORY SYSTEM
International Financial Reporting Standards (IFRS) Foundation

The IFRS Foundation (formerly known as the International Accounting Standards Committee Foundation (IASC)) is the supervisory body for the IASB and is responsible for governance issues and ensuring each member body is properly funded.

The principal objectives of the IFRS Foundation are to:

- develop a set of high quality, understandable, enforceable and globally accepted financial reporting standards
- promote the use and rigorous application of those standards
- to take account of the financial reporting needs of emerging economies and small and medium sized entities
- bring about the convergence of national and international financial reporting standards.

International Accounting Standards Board (IASB)

The IASB is the independent standard setting body of the IFRS foundation. Its members are responsible for the development and publication of IFRSs and interpretations developed by the IFRS IC. Upon its creation the IASB also adopted all existing International Accounting Standards.

All of the most important national standard setters are represented on the IASB and their views are taken into account so that a consensus can be reached. All national standard setters can issue IASB discussion papers and exposure drafts for comment in their own countries, so that the views of all preparers and users of financial statements can be represented. Each major national standard setter 'leads' certain international standard-setting projects.

The IFRS Interpretations Committee (IFRS IC)

The IFRS IC reviews widespread accounting issues (in the context of IFRS) on a timely basis and provides authoritative guidance on these issues (IFRICs). Their meetings are open to the public and, similar to the IASB, they work closely with national standard setters.

The IFRS Advisory Council (IFRS AC)

The IFRS AC is the formal advisory body to the IASB and the IFRS Foundation. It is comprised of a wide range of members who are affected by the IASB's work. Their objectives include:

- advising the IASB on agenda decisions and priorities in the their work,
- informing the IASB of the views of the Council with regard to major standard-setting projects, and
- giving other advice to the IASB or to the Trustees.

Development of an IFRS

The procedure for the development of an IFRS is as follows:

- The IASB identifies a subject and appoints an advisory committee to advise on the issues.
- The IASB publishes an exposure draft for public comment, being a draft version of the intended standard.
- Following the consideration of comments received on the draft, the IASB publishes the final text of the IFRS.
- At any stage the IASB may issue a discussion paper to encourage comment.
- The publication of an IFRS, exposure draft or IFRIC interpretation requires the votes of at least eight of the 15 IASB members.

THE REGULATORY FRAMEWORK

The need for regulation

A regulatory framework for the preparation of financial statements is necessary for a number of reasons:

- To ensure that the needs of the users of financial statements are met with at least a basic minimum of information.
- To ensure that all the information provided in the relevant economic arena is both comparable and consistent. Given the growth in multinational companies and global investment this arena is an increasing international one.
- To increase users' confidence in the financial reporting process.
- To regulate the behaviour of companies and directors towards their investors.

Financial reporting standards on their own would not be sufficient to achieve these aims. In addition there must be some legal and market-based regulation.

National regulatory frameworks for financial reporting

There are many elements to the regulatory environment of accounting. A typical regulatory structure includes:

- National financial reporting standards
- National law
- Market regulations
- Security exchange rules.

For example; the UK has its own national financial reporting authority, the Accounting Standards Board (part of the Financial Reporting Council) that issues financial reporting standards in the UK. The main piece of legislation affecting businesses in the UK is the Companies Act 2006. However, there are also many other pieces of UK, EU and even US legislation (such as the Sarbanes Oxley Act) that affect accountability in the UK. There are also numerous industry specific regulatory systems that affect accounting in the UK, for example; the Financial Services Authority, whose aim is to achieve public accountability of the financial services industry. Finally, there are regulations provided by the London Stock Exchange for companies whose shares are quoted on this market

CHAPTER FIVE
INTERPRETATION OF FINANCIAL STATEMENTS

Introduction

Financial statements on their own are of limited use. For example: if you were to identify that a business has made profits of $1 million what does that tell you about the business? Does it suggest the business is a success? It might, but not if in the previous year they made profits of $50 million and their closest rival earned profits of $60 million.

It is important that users of financial statements can interpret the financial statements to be able to draw out valid conclusions. Typically this involves the use of comparisons to prior years, forecasts and competitors. Users can compare sales and expense figures, asset and liability balances and cash flows to perform this analysis.

Ratio analysis is widely used to support this process of comparison. Don't forget though that ratios are calculated using the figures already present in the financial statements. The raw data is equally useful when performing analysis. Ratios are simply a tool to try and assist understanding and comparison.

Users of financial statements

When interpreting financial statements it is important to ascertain who are the users of accounts and what information they need:

- shareholders and potential investors – primarily concerned with receiving an adequate return on their investment, but also with the stability/liquidity of the business
- suppliers and lenders – concerned with the security of their debt or loan
- management – concerned with the trend and level of profits, since this is the main measure of their success.

Other potential users include:

- financial institutions
- employees
- professional advisors to investors
- financial journalists and commentators.

Ratio analysis

Ratios use simple calculations based upon the interactions in sets of data. For example; changes in costs of sale are directly linked to changes in sales activity. Changes in sales activity also have an effect upon wages and salaries, receivables, inventory levels etc. Ratios allow us to see those interactions in a simple, concise format.

Ratios are of limited use on their own, thus, the following points should serve as a useful checklist if you need to analyse data and comment on it:

- What does the ratio literally mean?
- What does a change in the ratio mean?
- What is the norm?
- What are the limitations of the ratio?

Focus of analysis

Traditionally financial statements analysis focuses on four key areas:

- profitability,
- liquidity,
- efficiency, and
- financial position.

EFFICIENCY ANALYSIS

This is similar to liquidity analysis in that it assess current assets and liabilities. The purpose of efficiency analysis, however, is to identify how effectively/efficiently management uses its resources (or working capital) to run the business.

Inventory turnover period
This is calculated as:

Inventory / cost of sales x 365
This simply measures how efficiently management uses its inventory to produce and sell goods.
An increasing number of days implies that management are holding onto inventory for longer. This could indicate lack of demand or poor inventory control.
Alternatively, the increase in inventory holding could be due to:
- buying bulk to take advantage of trade discounts
- reducing the risk of "stockouts," or
- an expected increase in orders.

Either way, the consequence is that the costs of storing, handling and insuring inventory levels will also increase. There is also an increased risk of inventory damage and obsolescence.

Alternative
An alternative is to express the inventory turnover period as a number of times:

Cost of sales / inventory = times p.a. the average inventory is consumed

A high turnover indicates that management generally hold quite a low level of inventory in comparison to overall sales. This means their costs of holding inventory are reduced, although they may need more frequent deliveries. A just in time system would reflect this sort of strategy. A low inventory turnover indicates that management hold on to a high level of inventory in comparison to overall sales levels.

A word of caution
Year-end inventory is normally used in the calculation of inventory turnover. An average (based on the average of year-start and year-end inventories) may be used to have a smoothing effect, although this may dampen the effect of a major change in the period. Inventory turnover ratios vary enormously with the nature of the business. For example, a fishmonger selling fresh fish would have an inventory turnover period of 1–2 days, whereas a building contractor may have an inventory turnover period of 200 days. Manufacturing

companies may have an inventory turnover ratio of 60–100 days; this period is likely to increase as the goods made become larger and more complex.

For large and complex items (e.g. rolling stock or aircraft) there may be sharp fluctuations in inventory turnover according to whether delivery took place just before or just after the year end.

A manufacturer should take into consideration:

- reliability of suppliers: if the supplier is unreliable it is prudent to hold more raw materials
- demand: if demand is erratic it is prudent to hold more finished goods.

Receivables collection period

This is normally expressed as a number of days: ***Trade receivables / credit sales x 365***

The ratio shows, on average, how long it takes to collect cash from credit customers once they have purchased goods. The collection period should be compared with:

- the stated credit policy
- previous period figures.

Increasing accounts receivables collection period is usually a bad sign suggesting lack of proper credit control which may lead to irrecoverable debts.

It may, however, be due to:

- a deliberate policy to attract more trade, or
- a major new customer being allowed different terms.

Falling receivables days is usually a good sign, though it could indicate that the company is suffering a cash shortage.

The trade receivables used may be a year-end figure or the average for the year. Where an average is used to calculate the number of days, the ratio is the average number of days' credit taken by customers.

For many businesses total sales revenue can safely be used, because cash sales will be insignificant. But cash-based businesses like supermarkets make the substantial majority of their sales for cash, so the receivables period should be calculated by reference to credit sales only.

The result should be compared with the stated credit policy. A period of 30 days or 'at the end of the month following delivery' is common credit terms.

The receivables days' ratio can be distorted by:

- using year-end figures which do not represent average receivables
- factoring of accounts receivables which results in very low trade receivables
- Sales on unusually long credit terms to some customers.

Payables payment period

This is usually expressed as: ***Trade payables / credit purchases x 365***

This represents the credit period taken by the company from its suppliers.

The ratio is always compared to previous years:

- A long credit period may be good as it represents a source of free finance.
- A long credit period may indicate that the company is unable to pay more quickly because of liquidity problems.

If the credit period is long:
- the company may develop a poor reputation as a slow payer and may not be able to find new suppliers
- existing suppliers may decide to discontinue supplies
- the company may be losing out on worthwhile cash discounts.

In most sets of basic financial statements the figure for purchases will not be available therefore cost of sales is normally used as an approximation in the calculation of the accounts payable payment period.

FINANCIAL POSITION ANALYSIS

When assessing the financial position of a business the main focus is its stability and exposure to risk. This is typically assessed by considering the way the business is structured and financed. This is referred to as gearing.

In simple terms gearing is a measure of the level of external debt a company has (e.g. outstanding loans) in comparison to equity finance (i.e. share capital and reserves).

Measuring gearing

There are two methods commonly used to express gearing as follows.

Debt/equity ratio:

This is calculated as: *Long-term debt / equity x 100*

Percentage of capital employed represented by borrowings:

This is calculated as: *Long-term debt / (equity + long-term debt) x 100*

Long term debt includes non-current loan and redeemable preference share liabilities. Equity includes share capital (and premium) balances plus reserves (revaluation reserve, retained earnings).

NB: redeemable preference shares are treated as liabilities because they must be repaid and are therefore debts of the company. Irredeemable preference shares do not have to be repaid and are therefore treated the same as ordinary shares and included in equity.

HIGH AND LOW GEARING

Risk

External debt finance is considered to be risky because there are mandatory, fixed repayment obligations. Failure to repay these amounts could lead to insolvency proceedings against the company.

Equity finance is less risky because there are no mandatory repayment obligations to shareholders. Failure to pay a dividend would not lead to insolvency proceedings.

Servicing of finance

The costs of servicing equity finance are generally considered to be higher than servicing external debt. This is because equity holders expect a greater return than they could achieve offering a fixed loan to a company. Remember lenders received fixed, mandatory repayments. They also take out security on the assets of a company. Equity holders do not have this comfort blanket; they get no guaranteed returns and they take on considerable risks. They would therefore expect greater returns on their investments; if they could not achieve this they would surely not accept the risk of buying shares and lend their money instead. Therefore highly geared companies (high level of debt to equity) are considered to be riskier but comparatively cheaper to service than lower geared companies (and vice versa).

Low-geared businesses also tend to provide scope to increase borrowings when potentially profitable projects are available as they are generally perceived to be less risky by banks and can therefore borrow more easily.

Interest cover

This is calculated as: ***Profit before interest and tax / interest payable***

Interest cover indicates the ability of a company to pay interest out of profits generated:

- low interest cover indicates to shareholders that their dividends are at risk (because most profits are eaten up by interest payments) and
- the company may have difficulty financing its debts if its profits fall
- interest cover of less than two is usually considered unsatisfactory.

A business must have a sufficient level of long-term capital to finance its long-term investment in non-current assets. Part of the investment in current assets would usually be financed by relatively permanent capital with the balance being provided by credit from suppliers and other short-term borrowings. Any expansion in activity will normally require a broadening of the long-term capital base, without which 'overtrading' may develop (see below).

Suitability of finance is also a key factor. A permanent expansion of a company's activities should not be financed by temporary, short-term borrowings. On the other hand, a short-term increase in activity such as the 'January sales' in a retail trading company could ideally be financed by overdraft.

A major addition to non-current assets such as the construction of a new factory would not normally be financed on a long-term basis by overdraft. It might be found, however, that the expenditure was temporarily financed by short-term loans until construction was completed, when the overdraft would be 'funded' by a long-term borrowing secured on the completed building.

LIQUIDITY ANALYSIS

These ratios assess the liquidity/solvency of a business (i.e. the ability to meet debt obligations) and how efficiently the company manages its working capital resources.

Current ratio

Current or working capital ratio: ***Current assets / current liabilities.***

This is usually presented as a ratio in the format of '4:1.'

The current ratio measures the adequacy of current assets to meet liabilities as they fall due. A high or increasing figure may appear safe but should be regarded with suspicion as it may be due to:

- high levels of inventory and receivables (this could mean inventory is unsaleable or that credit control is weak)

- high cash levels which could be put to better use (e.g. by investing in non-current assets).

Traditionally, a current ratio of 2:1 or higher was regarded as appropriate for most businesses to maintain creditworthiness. However, more recently a figure of 1.5:1 is regarded as the norm.

The current ratio should be, however, looked at in the light of what is normal for the business. For example, supermarkets tend to have low current ratios because:

- there are few trade receivables
- there is a high level of trade payables
- there is usually very tight cash control, to fund investment in developing new sites and improving sites.

It is also worth considering:

- availability of further finance, e.g. is the overdraft at the limit? – very often this information is highly relevant but is not disclosed in the accounts
- seasonal nature of the business – one way of doing this is to compare the interest charges in the income statement with the overdraft and other loans in the statement of financial position; if the interest rate appears abnormally high, this is probably because the company has had higher levels of borrowings during the year
- long-term liabilities, when they fall due and how will they be financed
- nature of the inventory – where inventories are slow moving, the quick ratio probably provides a better indicator of short-term liquidity.

Quick ratio

This is calculated as: ***Current assets - inventory / current liabilities***

The quick ratio is also known as the acid test ratio because by eliminating inventory from current assets it provides the acid test of whether the company has sufficient liquid resources (receivables and cash) to settle its liabilities.

Normal levels for the quick ratio range from 1:1 to 0.7:1.

Like the current ratio it is relevant to consider the nature of the business (again supermarkets have very low quick ratios).

Sometimes the quick ratio is calculated on the basis of a six-week time-frame (i.e. the quick assets are those which will turn into cash in six weeks; quick liabilities are those which fall due for payment within six weeks). This basis would usually include the following in quick assets:

- bank, cash and short-term investments
- trade receivables.

thus excluding prepayments and inventory.

Quick liabilities would usually include:

- bank overdraft which is repayable on demand
- trade payables, tax and social security
- dividends.

Income tax liabilities may be excluded.

When interpreting the quick ratio, care should be taken over the status of the bank overdraft. A company with a low quick ratio may actually have no problem in paying its amounts due if sufficient overall overdraft facilities are available.

PROFITABILITY ANALYSIS

Profitability analysis is aimed at understanding the performance of a business over time with regard to specific performance measurement criteria.

Gross profit margin

On a unit basis the gross profit represents the difference between the unit sales price and the direct cost per unit. The margin works this out on an average basis across all sales for the year.

Gross profit margin is calculated as follows: ***Gross profit / sales revenue x 100***

Changes in this ratio may be attributable to:

- selling prices
- product mix
- purchase costs
- production costs
- inventory valuations

Comparing gross profit margin over time

If gross profit has not increased in line with sales revenue, you need to establish why not. Is the discrepancy due to:

- increased 'purchase' costs: if so, are the costs under the company's control (i.e. does the company manufacture the goods sold)?
- inventory write-offs (likely where the company operates in a volatile marketplace, such as fashion retail)? or
- other costs being allocated to cost of sales – for example, research and development (R&D) expenditure?

Inter-company comparison of gross profit margin

Inter-company comparison of margins can be very useful but it is especially important to look at businesses within the same sector. For example, food retailing is able to support low margins because of the high volume of sales. Jewellers would usually need higher margins to offset lower sales volumes.

Low margins usually suggest poor performance but may be due to expansion costs (launching a new product) or trying to increase market share. Lower margins than usual suggest scope for improvement.

Above-average margins are usually a sign of good management although unusually high margins may make the competition keen to join in and enjoy the 'rich pickings'.

Operating profit margin (net profit)

The operating profit margin or net profit margin is calculated as:

Profit before interest and tax / sales revenue x 100

The operating margin is an expansion of the gross margin and includes all of the items that come after gross profit but before finance charges and taxation, such as selling and distribution costs and administration costs.

If the gross margin is a measure of how profitably a company can produce and sell its products and services the operating margin also measures how effectively the business manages/administers that process.

Therefore, if the gross margin has remained static but the operating margin has changed consider the following possibilities (these represent suggestions; it is not a comprehensive list):

- changes in employment patterns (recruitment, redundancy etc)
- changes to depreciation due to large acquisitions or disposals
- significant write-offs of irrecoverable debt
- changes in rental agreements
- significant investments in advertising
- rapidly changing fuel costs.

The operating margin is affected by more factors than the gross profit margin but it is equally useful to users and if the company does not disclose cost of sales it may be used on its own in lieu of the gross profit percentage.

One of the many factors affecting the trading profit margin is depreciation, which is open to considerable subjective judgement. Inter-company comparisons should be made after suitable adjustments to align accounting policies.

By the time you have reached operating (net) profit, there are many more factors to consider. If you are provided with a breakdown of expenses you can use this for further line-by-line comparisons. Bear in mind that:

- some costs are fixed or semi-fixed (e.g. property costs) and therefore not expected to change in line with revenue
- other costs are variable (e.g. packing and distribution, and commission).

Return on Capital Employed

ROCE is an important analysis tool as it allows users to assess how much profit the business generates from the capital invested in it. Profit margins of different companies are not necessarily comparable due to different sizes and business structures. You could have one company that makes large profits but based on huge levels of investment. Shareholders may decide they can make similar returns in different companies without such a high initial investment required.

In simple terms ROCE measures how much operating profit is generated for every $1 capital invested in the business. It is calculated as follws:

Profit before interest and tax / capital employed x 100

Capital employed is measured as equity, plus interest-bearing finance, i.e. non-current loans plus share capital and reserves.

Once calculated, ROCE should be compared with:

- previous years' figures – provided there have been no changes in accounting policies, or suitable adjustments have been made to facilitate comparison (note, however that

the effect of not replacing non-current assets is that their value will decrease and ROCE will increase)
- the company's target ROCE – where the company's management has determined a target return as part of its budget procedure, consistent failure by a part of the business to meet the target may make it a target for disposal
- other companies in same industry – care is required in interpretation, because of the possibility, noted above, of different accounting policies, ages of plant, etc.

The ratio also shows how efficiently a business is using its resources. If the return is very low, the business may be better off realising its assets and investing the proceeds in a high interest bank account! (This may sound extreme, but should be considered particularly for a small, unprofitable business with valuable assets such as property.) Furthermore, a low return can easily become a loss if the business suffers a downturn.

Net asset turnover
This is calculated as:

$$Sales\ revenue\ /\ capital\ employed = times\ p.a.$$

It measures management's efficiency in generating revenue from the net assets at its disposal. This is similar to ROCE but in this case we measure the amount of sales revenue generated for every $1 capital invested in the business. Generally speaking, the higher the ratio the more efficient the business is.

Be aware that both ROCE and asset turnover can be significantly affected by a change in the business structure. For example; imagine that a manufacturing company buys a significant amount of property and plant in a year with the aim to increasing production and therefore sales. The short term affect is that ROCE and asset turnover will initially fall but this does not mean the business is actually performing any worse. It may even be an indication of future gains.

The reason is that the capital balance (net assets) will increase in comparison to the steady sales figures of the business. It cannot be expected that a business can buy new assets and simply grow immediately. It would take a number of years for a business to grow into their new assets and increase production until they operated at 100% capacity. Even if they could instantly use 100% of the new facilities it is unlikely that they will simply be able to sell all the new goods they produce instantly. They will have to find new customers, perhaps in new markets to sell them to. Of course, this does not take into account competitor responses!

In summary; the increase in capital would be both significant and instant. The consequent improvement in performance would take longer to achieve and would most likely be spread over a number of years. Both ROCE and asset turnover would fall instantly and then start to improve each year as revenues start to grow.

Relationship between ratios
ROCE can be subdivided into operating profit margin and asset turnover.

$$Operating\ margin\ x\ asset\ turnover = ROCE$$

Profit margin is often seen as an indication of the quality of products or services supplied (top-of-range products usually have higher margins).

Asset turnover is often seen as a measure of how intensively the assets are worked or how efficiently they are used to generate revenue.

A trade-off often exists between margin and asset turnover that means different businesses can actually achieve the same ROCE:

- Low-margin businesses (e.g. food retailers) often have intensive asset usage (i.e. they produce a high volume of goods to sell but sell them at low prices).
- Higher margin businesses (e.g. luxury jewellery items) produce less goods but sell them at a high price. Many of these businesses still use very labour intensive, rather than machine intensive, methods of production. Such crafts are highly valued and consumers are willing to pay a premium for them.

CHAPTER SIX
THE FINANCIAL REPORTING SYSTEM

Objective of financial reporting

The main objective is to provide financial information about the reporting entity to users of the financial statements that is useful in making decisions about providing resources to the entity, as well as other financial decisions. That financial information includes a summary of the transactions of the business of a period of time, usually twelve months.

In order to effectively report that information the users a system must be established that can capture data about the relevant transactions and events that occur during the financial year, summarise them appropriately and present them in a format that the users are capable of understanding. This is the financial reporting system.

The system is also used to monitor the effectiveness of the business and to help conclude relevant transactions (for example; many goods/services are sold on credit, giving the customer a number of days/months to settle their debt. Credit control requires information from the accounting system with regard to who has not settled their debts and, for that reason, which needs to be chased for payment).

The information flow

The flow of information from the initial transaction to the financial statements is illustrated as follows:

- data is received about the transaction or event,
- the transaction or event is recorded in a book of prime entry,
- the summary totals from the books of prime entry are posted in the ledger accounts,
- the ledger account balances are summarised in a trial balance, and
- the trial balance totals are transferred to the financial statements.

Balancing and Closing a Ledger Account

Balancing off a ledger account

Once the transactions for a period have been recorded, it will be necessary to find the balance on the ledger account:

(1)Total both sides of the T account and find the larger total.

(2)Put the larger total in the total box on the debit and credit side.

(3)Insert a balancing figure to the side of the T account which does not currently add up to the amount in the total box. Call this balancing figure 'balance c/f' (carried forward) or 'balance c/d' (carried down).

(4)Carry the balance down diagonally and call it 'balance b/f' (brought forward) or 'balance b/d' (brought down).

Illustration

A company has the following ledger account at the period end:

Cash			
	$		$
Capital	10,000	Purchases	200
Sales	250	Rent	150
		Electricity	75

It would be balanced off as follows:

Cash			
	$		$
Capital	10,000	Purchases	200
Sales	250	Rent	150
		Electricity	75
		Balance c/f	9,825
	10,250		10,250
Balance b/f	9,825		

Closing a ledger account

At the year end, the ledger accounts must be closed off in preparation for the recording of transactions in the next accounting period. Statement of financial position

Ledger Accounts

Assets/liabilities at the end of a period = assets/liabilities at start of the next period, e.g. the cash at bank at the end of one day will be the cash at bank at the start of the following day. Balancing the account will result in:

- a balance c/f (being the asset/liability at the end of the accounting period)
- a balance b/f (being the asset/liability at the start of the next accounting period). These are left as they are as an opening figure that next period's transactions and events can follow on from. Income statement

Ledger Accounts

At the end of a period any amounts that relate to that period are transferred out of the income and expenditure accounts into another ledger account called the income statement. This is done by closing the account.

There should be no balances carried forward to the next accounting period for income statement items.

BOOKS OF PRIME ENTRY
Introduction
The ledger accounts of a business are the main source of information used to prepare the financial statements. However, if a business were to update their ledgers each time a transaction occurred, the ledger accounts would quickly become cluttered and errors might be made. This would also be a very time consuming process.

To avoid this complication, all transactions are initially recorded in a book of prime entry. This is a simple note of the transaction, the relevant customer/supplier and the amount of the transaction. It is, in essence, a long list of daily transactions.

Different types of book
Several books of prime entry exist, each recording a different type of transaction:

Book of prime entry	Transaction type
Sales day book	Credit sales
Purchases day book	Credit purchases
Sales returns day book	Returns of goods sold on credit
Purchases returns day book	Returns of goods bought on credit
Cash book	All bank transactions
Petty cash book	All small cash transactions
The journal	All transactions not recorded elsewhere

The sum total of the day's transactions is recorded in the accounting ledgers of the company. This is done in a 'double entry' format.

The sales day book
The sales book summarises the daily sales made on credit terms (i.e. the goods are sold and payment is collected at a later date).

Date	Invoice	Customer	Ledger Ref	$
4.1.X6	1	Jake	RL3	4,500
4.1.X6	2	Bella	RL18	3,000
4.1.X6	3	Fizz	RL6	2,200
4.1.X6	4	Milo	RL1	10,000
4.1.X6	5	Max	RL12	500

Total for 4.1.X6   20,200

The total sales for the day of $20,200 will be entered into the accounting ledgers in double entry format.

Purchases day book

The purchase day book summarises the daily purchases made on credit terms (i.e. the goods are purchased and payment is made at a later date).

Date	Invoice	Customer	Ledger Ref	$
4.1.X6	34	Harry	PL2	2,700
4.1.X6	11	Ron	PL37	145
4.1.X6	5609	Hermione	PL12	4,675
4.1.X6	2	Neville	PL9	750
4.1.X6	577	Draco	PL1	345
Total for 4.1.X6				8,615

The total purchases for the day of $8,615 will be entered into the accounting ledgers in double entry format.

The sales returns day book

Date	Invoice	Customer	Ledger Ref	$
4.1.X6	1	Max	RL12	50
4.1.X6	2	Ernie	RL2	450
4.1.X6	3	Pat	RL20	390
4.1.X6	4	Sam	RL27	670
4.1.X6	5	Milo	RL1	2,300
Total for 4.1.X6				3,860

The purchases returns day book

Date	Invoice	Customer	Ledger Ref	$
4.1.X6	112	Harry	PL3	600
4.1.X6	56	Cho	PL16	75
4.1.X6	7	Fleur	PL2	800
4.1.X6	890	Neville	PL1	50
4.1.X6	12	Draco	PL12	100
Total for 4.1.X6				1,625

The cash book

All transactions involving cash at bank are recorded in the cash book. Many businesses have two distinct cash books: a **cash payments book** and a **cash receipts book.**

A note of cash discounts given and received is also recorded in the cash book. This is to facilitate the recording of discounts in both the general and accounts payable/receivable ledgers.

It is common for businesses to use a columnar format cash book in order to analyse types of cash payment and receipt.

Illustrative cash payments book
The following is the cash payments book of a small business.

Date	Detail	Bank	Discount	ledger Payables	Rent
		$	$	$	$
18.7.X6	Mr A	1,400	100	1,400	
18.7.X6	Office	3,000			3,000
18.7.X6	Mr B	210		210	
18.7.X6	Mr C	1,600	80	1,600	
18.7.X6	Shop	400			400
		6,610	180	3,210	3,400

The Journal
The journal is a book of prime entry which records transactions which are not routine (and not recorded in any other book of prime entry), for example:
- year-end adjustments
    - depreciation charge for the year
    - irrecoverable debt write-off
    - record the movement in the allowance for receivables
    - accruals and prepayments
    - closing inventory
    - acquisitions and disposals of non-current assets
- opening balances for statement of financial position items
- correction of errors.

The journal is a clear and comprehensible way of setting out a bookkeeping double entry that is to be made.

Presentation of a journal
A journal should be laid out in the following way:
Dr Non-current asset $xxx
Cr Payables $xxx
A brief narrative should be given to explain the entry.

BUSINESS TRANSACTIONS AND DOCUMENTATION

In every business a number of transactions and events will take place every day. The role of financial reporting is to effectively measure the effects of those transactions and events, record the effects on the business and summarise those transactions and their consequences in a format that is useful to the users of the financial statements.

The main transactions that take place include sales, purchases (of goods and of services) and payroll related transactions. Others include rental costs, raising finance, repayment of finance, and taxation related costs to name but a few. All of these transactions must be adequately captured by the financial reporting system.

With most transactions a supporting document will be created to confirm the transaction has taken place, when the transaction took place and the associated value of the transaction. This documentation is vital to the financial accountant, who uses the information on the documents as a data source to initiate the measurement and recording of the transactions. The table below summarises the main types of business documentation and sources of data for an accounting system, together with their content and purpose.

	Contents	Purpose
Quotation	Quantity/description/details of goods required.	To establish price from various suppliers and cross refer to purchase requisition.
Purchase order	Details of supplier, e.g. name, address. Quantity/ description/details of goods required and price. Terms and conditions of delivery, payment, etc.	Sent to supplier as request for supply. To check to the quotation and delivery note.
Sales order	Quantity/description/details of goods required and price.	Cross checked with the order placed by customer. Sent to the stores/ warehouse department for processing of the order.
Despatch note (goods despatched note – GDN)	Details of supplier, e.g. name and address. Quantity and description of goods	Provided by supplier. Checked with goods received and purchase order.
Goods received note (GRN)	Quantity and description of goods.	Produced by company receiving the goods as proof of receipt. Matched with delivery note and purchase order.
Invoice	Name and address of supplier and customer; details of goods, e.g. quantity, price, value, sales tax, terms of credit, etc.	Issued by supplier of goods as a request for payment. For the supplier selling the goods/services this will be treated as a sales invoice. For the customer this will be treated as a purchase invoice.
Statement	Details of supplier, e.g. name and address. Has details of date, invoice numbers and values,	Issued by the supplier. Checked with other documents to ensure that the amount owing is correct.

	payments made, refunds, amount owing.	
Credit note	Details of supplier, e.g. name and address. Contains details of goods returned, e.g. quantity, price, value, sales tax, terms of credit, etc.	Issued by the supplier. Checked with documents regarding goods returned.
Debit note	Details of the supplier. Contains details of goods returned, e.g. quantity, price, value, sales tax, terms of credit, etc.	Issued by the company receiving the goods. Cross referred to the credit note issued by the supplier.
Remittance advice	Method of payment, invoice number, account number, date, etc.	Sent to supplier with, or as notification of, payment.
Receipt	Details of payment received.	Issued by the selling company indicating the payment received.

The above list is based upon the documents created by a traditional manufacturing company. Not all companies will produce all of these documents. In the same manner some companies may produce alternative forms of documentation, particularly if they operate in the services industry or overseas

LEDGER ACCOUNTS

Definition
In simple terms the ledger accounts are where the double entry records of all transactions and events are made. They are the principal books or files for recording and totalling monetary transactions by account. A company's financial statements are generated from summary totals in the ledgers.

The division of the ledger
In most companies each class of transaction and their associated assets and liabilities are given their own account. For example, there will be separate accounts for sales, purchases, rent, insurance costs, cash assets, inventory assets, liabilities to pay suppliers (payables), amounts due from customers (receivables) etc. There is no rule as to how many accounts a business should have but the system should facilitate effective and efficient accounting and control. Each account in the system is referred to as a 'ledger.'

The general ledger
The term 'general ledger' is used to refer to the overall system of ledger accounts within a business. It is sometimes referred to as the 'nominal' ledger. It houses all the separate ledgers required to produce a complete trial balance and, consequently, set of financial statements.

Ledgers as part of an accounting system

At the end of each day (or other period, as deemed appropriate) the totals from the day books are posted to the ledger accounts in double entry format.

As stated above, each class of transaction, asset, liability and item of equity will have it's own ledger account. The totals of each ledger will eventually be transferred onto a summary list of balances referred to as 'the trial balance.' Once the business has finalised their accounting controls the totals from the trial balance are transferred into the financial statements.

DOUBLE ENTRY BOOKKEEPING

Introduction

At the end of each trading period, usually a day, the total of the transactions recorded in the entry are transferred into the ledger accounts. The totals are recorded using a double entry format, which reflect the duality concept, i.e. each transaction has two effects on the entity.

The ledger accounts

Each class of transaction and event is recorded in its own account, called a ledger. These were traditionally drawn up manually as an enlarged 'T;' hence they are popularly referred to as T accounts.

The two sides of the T account were created to reflect the dual nature of transactions, with one side (the left) representing a debit entry and the other side (the right) representing a credit entry.

Ledger accounts are traditionally drawn up as illustrated below:

Debit (Dr)   **Credit (Cr)**

Name of account e.g. cash, sales

Date	Narrative	$	Date	Narrative	$

Debits and credits

Debits typically reflect an increase in business assets or the incurring of expenses.

Credits typically reflect an increase in business liabilities or the earning of income. Many mnemonics exist to aid learning this. One such example is 'PEARLS:'

Debit	Credit
Increase in: **P**urchases **E**xpenses **A**ssets	Increase in: **R**evenues **L**iabilities **S**hareholder's equity

It is important to note that the opposite is also true, for example; a reduction in assets would constitute a credit entry into the ledgers.

Steps to record a transaction
(1)Identify the items that are affected.
(2)Consider whether they are being increased or decreased.
(3)Decide whether each account should be debited or credited.
(4)Check that a debit entry and a credit entry have been made and they are both for the same amount.

RECORDING BASIC CASH TRANSACTIONS
Cash transactions
Cash transactions are those where payment is made or received immediately (i.e. when cash is exchanged at the point of sale/purchase). Sales and purchases made by cheque, however, are classed as cash transactions. The main reason for this is that traditionally such transactions would be processed using a cash register or cash till. The cheques and cash in the till would be counted at the end of the day and then transferred to the bank account.

Double entry for cash transactions
For the sake of simplicity the following illustrations all refer to payments and receipts of cash being made out of the "cash" account, rather than distinguishing between "bank ledgers" and "cash ledgers."
When cash is received (i.e. receipt of an asset) the entry in the cash ledger is a debit. When cash is paid out (i.e. a reduction in an asset) the entry in the cash ledger is a credit.

Illustration
A business conducts the following transactions
(1)It pays $80 for rent by cheque.
(2)It sells goods for $230 cash which he banks.
(3)It purchases $70 of goods for resale using cash.
(4)It sells more goods for cash, receiving $3,400.

The double entry journals for these transactions are as follows:
(1)Dr rental expenses $80
Cr cash $80
(2)Dr cash $230
Cr sales revenue $230
(3)Dr purchases $70
Cr cash $70
(4)Dr cash $3,400
Cr sales revenue $3,400

These are posted the ledger accounts as illustrated below:

Cash

	$		$
Sales (2)	230	Rent (1)	80
Sales (4)	3,400	Purchases (3)	70

Sales

	$		$
		Cash (2)	230
		Cash (4)	3,400

Rent

	$		$
Cash (1)	80		

Purchases

	$		$
Cash (3)	70		

RECORDING CREDIT TRANSACTIONS

Introduction
Credit sales and purchases are transactions where goods or services change hands immediately, but payment is not made or received until sometime in the future.
Money that a business is owed is accounted for in the receivables ledger.
Money that a business owes is accounted for in the payables ledger.

Illustration
A business conducts the following transactions:
(1)Sell goods for cash for $60.
(2)Pay insurance premium by cheque – $400.
(3)Sell goods for $250 – the customer will pay in a month.
(4)Pay $50 petrol for the delivery van.
(5)Buy $170 goods for resale on credit.
(6)Buys $57 of goods for resale, paying by cheque.
(7)Buy another $40 goods for resale, paying cash.
(7)Buy a new computer for the business for $800.

These transactions are recorded in the ledger accounts as follows:

Cash

	$		$
Sales (1)	60	Insurance (2)	400
		Motor expenses (4)	50
		Purchases (6)	57
		Purchases (7)	40
		Non-current assets (8)	800

Sales

	$		$
		Bank (1)	60
		Receivables (3)	250

Insurance (expense)

	$		$
Bank (2)	400		

Receivables

	$		$
Sales (3)	250		

Motor expenses

	$		$
Bank (4)	50		

Purchases

	$		$
Payables (5)	170		
Cash (6)	57		
Cash (7)	40		

Payables

	$		$
		Purchases (5)	170

Non-current asset computer)		
	$	$
Bank (8)	800	

THE ACCOUNTING EQUATION

Duality

Each transaction that a business enters into affects the financial statements in two ways.
For example; a business buys a vehicle for cash. The two effects on the business are:

- It has increased the vehicle assets it has at its disposal for generating income, and
- There is a decrease in cash available to the business.

As another example let's assume a business sells goods on credit. The two effects on the business are:

- The business has generated sales income, and
- The business is owed cash from its customer (called a receivable).

If the principles of duality are followed the accounting equation should always balance.

Double entry bookkeeping

The application of duality is double entry bookkeeping; whenever a transaction occurs both of the effects on the business must be recorded in the ledger accounts in order to maintain the accounting equation in the financial statements.

The two financial effects are recorded with one as a 'debit' and the other as a 'credit' to reflect the equal and opposite nature of the effects on the business.

REFERENCE

Abbott, L. J., S. Parker and T. J. Presley. 2012. Female board presence and the likelihood of financial restatement. *Accounting Horizons* (December): 607-629.

Abdel-Khalik, A. R. 1975. Advertising effectiveness and accounting policy. *The Accounting Review* (October): 657-670. (JSTOR link).

Abdel-Khalik, A. R. and J. C. Mckeown. 1978. Disclosure of estimates of holding gains and the assessment of systematic risk. *Journal of Accounting Research*(Studies on Changes in General and Specific Prices): 46-77. (JSTOR link).

Abdel-Khalik, A. R. and J. C. McKeown. 1978. [Discussion of disclosure of estimates of holding gains and the assessment of systematic risk]: A reply. *Journal of Accounting Research* (Studies on Changes in General and Specific Prices): 106-110. (JSTOR link).

Abdel-Khalik, A. R. and J. Espejo. 1978. Expectations data and the predictive value of interim reporting. *Journal of Accounting Research* (Spring): 1-13. (JSTOR link).

Abdel-Khalik, A. R., P. R. Graul and J. D. Newton. 1986. Reporting uncertainty and assessment of risk: Replication and extension in a Canadian setting. *Journal of Accounting Research* (Autumn): 372-382. (JSTOR link).

Abdelsalam, O. H., S. M. Bryant and D. L. Street. 2007. An examination of the comprehensiveness of corporate internet reporting provided by London-listed companies. *Journal of International Accounting Research* 6(2): 1-33.

Abdolmohammadi, M. J. and W. J. Read. 2010. Corporate governance ratings and financial restatements: Pre and Post Sarbanes-Oxley Act. *Journal of Forensic & Investigative Accounting* 2(1): 1-44.

Aboody, D. and B. Lev. 1998. The value relevance of intangibles: The case of software capitalization. *Journal of Accounting Research* (Studies on Enhancing the Financial Reporting Model): 161-191. (JSTOR link).

Aboody, D. and R. Kasznik. 2000. CEO stock option awards and the timing of corporate voluntary disclosures. *Journal of Accounting and Economics* (February): 73-100.

Aboody, D., M. E. Barth and R. Kasznik. 1999. Revaluations of fixed assets and future firm performance: Evidence from the UK. *Journal of Accounting and Economics* (January): 149-178.

Aboody, D., M. E. Barth and R. Kasznik. 2004. Firms' voluntary recognition of stock-based compensation expense. *Journal of Accounting Research* (May): 123-150. (JSTOR link).

Aboody, D., R. Kasznik and M. Williams. 2000. Purchase versus pooling in stock-for-stock acquisitions: Why do firms care? *Journal of Accounting and Economics*(June): 261-286.

Accounting Principles Board. 1978. Basic Concepts and Accounting Principles Underlying Financial Statements of Business Enterprises. In *Professional Standards, Accounting, Current Text*. Commerce Clearing House.

Adams, B. 2002. Creating value with instant close. *Strategic Finance* (September): 48-51. (Related to ERP systems).

Adams, C. A. and K. J. McPhail. 2004. Reporting and the politics of difference: (Non)disclosure on ethnic minorities. *Abacus* 40(3): 405-435.

Adams, E. E. 1922. Provision for obsolescence. *Journal of Accountancy* (May): 387-388.

Adelberg, A. H. 1979. A methodology for measuring the understandability of financial report messages. *Journal of Accounting Research* (Autumn): 565-592. (JSTOR link).

Adler, J. 2010. Are your account reconciliations accurate? *Strategic Finance* (May): 42-46. ("Account reconciliation: A report that assesses the validity, correctness, or appropriateness of an account balance at a specific point in time - documented by relevant calculations, clear and complete explanations, and copies of supporting documentation - and that is consistent with the company's policies and procedures.").

Adler, J. 2011. Closing the loop on closing the books. *Strategic Finance* (July): 43-47. *Advanced Corporate Reporting (ACCA) Textbook*. Foulks Lynch.

Aerts, W. 1994. On the use of accounting logic as an explanatory category in narrative accounting disclosures. *Accounting, Organizations and Society* 19(4-5): 337-353.

Agami, A. M. 1978. Accounting for troubled debt restructurings - a flowchart approach. *Management Accounting* (November): 51-55.

AICPA. 1975. *Statement on Auditing Standards No. 5: The Meaning of "Present Fairly in Conformity with Generally Accepted Accounting Principles" in the Independent Auditor's Report*. AICPA.

AICPA. 2004. *AICPA Professional Standards: As of June 1, 2004 (AICPA Professional Standards, 2004)*. AICPA.

AICPA. 2008. *FASB Codification Developments 2008*. AICPA.

AICPA. 2008. *Not-for-Profit Organizations Checklists & Illustrative Financial Statements*. AICPA.

AICPA. 2008. *State and Local Governments Checklists & Illustrative Financial Statements*. AICPA.

AICPA. 2009. *Current Economic Crisis: Accounting Issues and Risks for Financial Management and Reporting - 2009*. AICPA.

AICPA. 2012. *Current Accounting Issues and Risks for Financial Management and Reporting - 2012/13 Financial Reporting Alert*. AICPA.

AICPA. 2012. *U.S. GAAP Financial Statements - Best Practices in Presentation and Disclosure*. AICPA.

AICPA Study Group on the Objectives of Financial Statements. 1973. *Objectives of Financial Statements*. AICPA.

Aier, J. K., J. Comprix, M. T. Gunlock and D. Lee. 2005. The financial expertise of CFOs and accounting restatements. *Accounting Horizons* (September): 123-135.

Ajinkya, B. B. 1980. An empirical evaluation of line-of-business reporting. *Journal of Accounting Research* (Autumn): 343-361. (JSTOR link).

Akhtaruddin, M., M. A. Hossain, M. Hossain and L. Yao. 2009. Corporate governance and voluntary disclosure in corporate annual reports of Malaysian firms.*Journal of Applied Management Accounting Research* (Winter): 1-20.

Akresh, M. S. and J. Fuersich. 1994. Stock options: Accounting, valuation, and management issues. *Management Accounting* (March): 51-53.

Alali, F. and L. Cao. 2010. International financial reporting standards - credible and reliable? An overview. *Advances in Accounting: Incorporating Advances in International Accounting* 26(1): 79-86.

Alali, F. and S. Romero. 2012. The use of the Internet for corporate reporting in the Mercosur (Southern common market): The Argentina case. *Advances in Accounting: Incorporating Advances in International Accounting* 28(1): 157-167.

Albrecht, W. S. 1976. Estimation error in income determination. *The Accounting Review* (October): 823-837. (JSTOR link).

Albrecht, W. S. 1978. Estimation error in income determination: A reply. *The Accounting Review* (October): 1003-1004. (JSTOR link).

Alderman, C. W., G. E. Summers and M. J. Welsh. 1983. The trend toward soft data in accounting. *Management Accounting* (December): 34-35, 38-39.

Aldridge, C. R. and J. L. Colbert. 1997. We need better financial reporting. *Management Accounting* (July): 32-36. (Discussion of the need for nonfinancial and forward-looking information as well as financial and historical information).

Alexander, D. and E. Jermakowicz. 2006. A true and fair view of the principles/rules debate. *Abacus* 42(2): 132-164.

Alexander, M. O. 1981. Discussion of the SEC "reversal" of FASB Statement No 19: An investigation of information effects. *Journal of Accounting Research*(Studies on Standardization of Accounting Practices: An Assessment of Alternative Institutional Arrangements): 212-217. (JSTOR link).

Alexander, S. S. 1973. Income measurement in a dynamic economy. Monograph no 1. In *Five Monographs on Business Income*. AICPA. Reprint of the 1950 original. Scholars Book Co: 1-95.

Alford, A., J. Jones, R. Leftwich and M. Zmijewski. 1993. The relative informativeness of accounting disclosures in different countries. *Journal of Accounting Research* (Studies on International Accounting): 183-223. (JSTOR link).

Alford, R. M., T. M. DiMattia, N. T. Hill and K. T. Stevens. 2011. A series of revenue recognition research cases using the codification. *Issues In Accounting Education* (August): 609-618.

Alford, A. W., J. J. Jones and M. E. Zmijewski. 1994. Extensions and violations of the statutory SEC form 10-K filing requirements. *Journal of Accounting and Economics* (January): 229-254.

Alhashim, D. D. and S. P. Garner. 1973. Postulates for localized uniformity in accounting. *Abacus* 9(1): 62-72.

Ali, A. and K. R. Kumar. 1994. The magnitudes of financial statement effects and accounting choice: The case of the adoption of SFAS 87. *Journal of Accounting and Economics* (July): 89-114.

Ali, A. and L. Hwang. 2000. Country-specific factors related to financial reporting and the value relevance of accounting data. *Journal of Accounting Research*(Spring): 1-21. (JSTOR link).

Ali, A., T. Chen and S. Radhakrishnan. 2007. Corporate disclosures by family firms. *Journal of Accounting and Economics* (September): 238-286.

Alleman, R. H. 1982. Why ITT likes FAS 52. *Management Accounting* (July): 22-29.

Allen, L. E. 1958. Toward more clarity in business communications by modern logical methods. *Management Science* (October): 121-135. (JSTOR link).

Allen, R. 2005. Less is more. *Strategic Finance* (June): 44-49. (Improving the closing process).

Allen, R. N. 1950. Timely issuance of monthly reports - An outline of an early closing procedure. *N.A.C.A. Bulletin* (January): 637-642.

Alles, M. G. and G. L. Grey. 2012. A relative cost framework of demand for external assurance of XBRL filings. *Journal of Information Systems* (Spring): 103-126.

Alltizer, R. L., B. P. McAllister and B. D. Jarnagin. 2008. FIN 48: Accounting and auditing implications. *The CPA Journal* (August): 44-47.

Alm, I. W. 1939. Combining adjusting and closing Entries. *The Accounting Review* (December): 432-436. (JSTOR link).

Altamuro, J. and A. Beatty. 2010. How does internal control regulation affect financial reporting? *Journal of Accounting and Economics* (February): 58-74.

Amer, T. 1991. An experimental investigation of multi-cue financial information display and decision making. *Journal of Information Systems* (Fall): 18-34.

Amer, T., A. D. Bailey Jr. and P. De. 1987. A review of the computer information systems research related to accounting and auditing. *Journal of Information Systems* (Fall): 3-28.

Amernic, J., R. Craig and D. Tourish. 2012. Reflecting a company's safety culture in "fairly presented" financial statements: The case of BP. *The CPA Journal*(April): 6, 8-10.

Amernic, J. H. 1986. A framework for analyzing financial reporting cases. *Journal of Accounting Education* 4(1): 81-94.

Amir, E. 1996. The effect of accounting aggregation on the value-relevance of financial disclosures: The case of SFAS No. 106. *The Accounting Review* (October): 573-590. (JSTOR link).

Amir, E. and A. Ziv. 1997. Recognition, disclosure, or delay: Timing the adoption of SFAS No. 106. *Journal of Accounting Research* (Spring): 61-81. (JSTOR link).

Amlie, T. T. 2011. Measurement of incentive stock option expense: Is the issue settled? *The CPA Journal* (July): 28-31.

Anantharaman, D. 2012. Comparing self-regulation and statutory regulation: Evidence from the accounting profession. *Accounting, Organizations and Society*37(2): 55-77.

Andersen, A. 1929. Financial and industrial investigations. *The Accounting Review* (March): 16-22. (JSTOR link).

Anderson, A., P. Herring and A. Pawlicki. 2005. EBR: The next step. *Journal of Accountancy* (June): 71-74. (Enhanced business reporting).

Anderson, C. 2010. Discussion of 'Analyzing late SEC filings for differential impacts of IS and accounting issues'. *International Journal of Accounting Information Systems* 11(3): 211-213.

Anderson, J. A. 1976. *A Comparative Analysis of Selected Income Measurement Theories in Financial Accounting. Studies in Accounting Research* (12). American Accounting Association.

Anderson, J. A. 1982. A discussion of "Coalition formation in the APB and the FASB". *The Accounting Review* (January): 190-195. (JSTOR link).

Anderson, J. A. and S. L. Meyers. 1975. Some limitations of efficient markets research for the determination of financial reporting standards. *Abacus* 11(1): 18-36.

Anderson, J. C. and A. W. Frankle. 1980. Voluntary social reporting: An iso-beta portfolio analysis. *The Accounting Review* (July): 467-479. (JSTOR link).

Anderson, J. C. and J. G. Louderback III. 1975. Income manipulation and purchase-pooling: Some additional results. *Journal of Accounting Research* (Autumn): 338-343. (JSTOR link).

Anderson, R. C., S. A. Mansi and D. M. Reeb. 2004. Board characteristics, accounting report integrity, and the cost of debt. *Journal of Accounting and Economics*(September): 315-342.

Anderson, T. 1992. Accounting earnings announcements and differential predisclosure information. *Abacus* 28(2): 121-132.

Anderson, T. L. Jr. 1982. Do annual reports really communicate? *Management Accounting* (September): 15-21, 42.

Ang, N., B. K. Sidhu and N. Gallery. 2000. The incentives of Australian public companies lobbying against proposed superannuation accounting standards. *Abacus*36(1): 40-70.

Anthony, J. J. and S. C. Dilley. 1988. The tax basis financial reporting alternative for nonpublic firms. *Accounting Horizons* (September): 41-47.

Anthony, P. 1977. Goodbye goodwill - Hello share of the market. *Management Accounting* (June): 31-40.

Anthony, R. N. 1993. The foolishness of FASB's nonprofit classes. *Management Accounting* (July): 53-57.

Anthony, R. N. 1997. Financial reporting in the 1990s and beyond. *Accounting Horizons* (December): 107-111.

Anton, H. R. 1954. Funds statement practices in the United States and Canada. *The Accounting Review* (October): 620-627. (JSTOR link).

Anton, H. R. 1955. The funds statement as an internal report to management. *The Accounting Review* (January): 71-79. (JSTOR link).

Anton, H. R. 1973. Discussion of an empirical evaluation of possible explanations for the differing treatment of apparently similar unusual events. *Journal of Accounting Research* (Empirical Research in Accounting: Selected Studies): 96-98. (JSTOR link).

Anyon, J. T. 1909. Sinking funds and reserve accounts. *Journal of Accountancy* (January): 185-191.

Apitz, J. W. 1913. A question of partners' drawing and dividends. *Journal of Accountancy* (January): 72-73.

Apostolou, B. and N. G. Apostolou. 2008. Derivatives: New disclosures required. *The CPA Journal* (November): 28-36.

Appleby, B. G. 1946. Correlation of costs to financial statements. *The Accounting Review* (October): 410-415. (JSTOR link).

Aranya, N. 1974. The influence of pressure groups on financial statements in Britain. *Abacus* 10(1): 3-12.

Archambault, J. J. and M. Archambault. 2005. The effect of regulation on statement disclosures in the 1915 Moody's Manuals. *The Accounting Historians Journal*32(1): 1-22. (JSTOR link).

Archer, S., P. Del Vaille and S. Mcleay. 1996. A statistical model of international accounting harmonization. *Abacus* 32(1): 1-29.

Archerd, W. R. 1952. An application of whole dollar accounting. *N.A.C.A. Bulletin* (January): 617-628. (Discussion related to eliminating pennies - pennyless accounting, cents elimination, or whole dollar accounting).

Archibald, T. R. 1967. The return to straight-line depreciation: An analysis of a change in accounting method. *Journal of Accounting Research* (Empirical Research in Accounting: Selected Studies): 164-180. (JSTOR link).

Armstrong, C. S., W. R. Guay and J. P. Weber. 2010. The role of information and financial reporting in corporate governance and debt contracting. *Journal of Accounting and Economics* (December): 179-234.

Armstrong, R. D. 1920. Regulation of bond discount. *Journal of Accountancy* (July): 18-35.

Arndt, T. L. and R. W. Jones. 1982. Closing the GAAP in church accounting. *Management Accounting* (August): 26-31.

Arnett, H. E. 1965. Application of the capital gains and losses concept in practice. *The Accounting Review* (January): 54-64. (JSTOR link).

Arnett, H. E. 1967. The concept of fairness. *The Accounting Review* (April): 291-297. (JSTOR link).

Arnett, H. E. 1969. Taxable income vs. financial income: How much uniformity can we stand? *The Accounting Review* (July): 482-494. (JSTOR link).

Arnett, H. E. 1978. APB opinion no. 29: Accounting for nonmonetary transactions - Some new perspectives. *Management Accounting* (October): 41-48.

Arnett, H. E. 1979. *Proposed Funds Statements for Managers and Investors*. National Association of Accountants.

Arnold, D. F. and T. E. Humann. 1973. Earnings per share: An empirical test of the market parity and the investment value methods. *The Accounting Review*(January): 23-33. (JSTOR link).

Arnold, J. L., W. W. Holder and J. R. Williams. 1983. FASB should establish an accounting laboratory. *Management Accounting* (March): 52-54.

Arnold, P. J. and L. S. Oakes. 1998. Accounting as discursive construction: The relationship between statement of financial accounting standards no. 106 and the dismantling of retiree health benefits. *Accounting, Organizations and Society* 23(2): 129-153.

Arnold, S. 2009. IFRS risk planning and controls execution. *Journal of Accountancy* (September): 34-37.

Arya, A. and A. Reinstein. 2010. Recent developments in fair value accounting. *The CPA Journal* (August): 20-29.

Arya, A. and B. Mittendorf. 2004. Benefits of a slanted view: A discussion of 'disclosure bias'. *Journal of Accounting and Economics* (December): 251-262.

Arya, A., J. C. Glover and S. Sunder. 2003. Are unmanaged earnings always better for shareholders? *Accounting Horizons* (Supplement): 111-116.

Asare, S. K. and A. M. Wright. 2012. Investors', auditors', and lenders' understanding of the message conveyed by the standard audit report on the financial statements. *Accounting Horizons* (June): 193-217.

Asbra, M. and K. Miles. 2009. The valuation of earn-outs and acquired contingencies under SFAS 141(R). *The CPA Journal* (March): 38-42.

Ashbaugh, H. and M. Pincus. 2001. Domestic accounting standards, international accounting standards, and the predictability of earnings. *Journal of Accounting Research* (December): 417-434. (JSTOR link).

Ashbaugh, H., K. M. Johnstone and T. D. Warfield. 1999. Corporate reporting on the internet. *Accounting Horizons* (September): 241-257.

Ashburne, J. G. 1962. A forward looking statement of financial position. *The Accounting Review* (July): 475-478. (JSTOR link).

Ashton, R. H. 1974. The predictive-ability criterion and user prediction models. *The Accounting Review* (October): 719-732. (JSTOR link).

Ashton, R. H. 1976. The predictive-ability criterion and user prediction models: A reply. *The Accounting Review* (July): 680-682. (JSTOR link).

Asthana, S. 2001. The impact of regulatory and audit environment on managers' discretionary accounting choices: The case of SFAS No. 106. *Accounting and the Public Interest* (1): 73-96.

Atiase, R. K., L. S. Bamber and R. N. Freeman. 1988. Accounting disclosures based on company size: Regulations and capital markets evidence. *Accounting Horizons* (March): 18-26.

Atkins, R. 1917. Cost records and profits. *Journal of Accountancy* (September): 239-240.

Atkinson, S. K. 1935. Accounting treatment of the bond sinking fund and reserve. *The Accounting Review* (March): 102-105. (JSTOR link).

Atkinson, S. K. 1953. For better public reporting of production costs. *N.A.C.A. Bulletin* (August): 1575-1587.

www.ingramcontent.com/pod-product-compliance
Lightning Source LLC
Chambersburg PA
CBHW040829180526
45159CB00001B/122